From See

The Most Accurate Guide to Understanding and Growing Marijuana for Medical and Recreational Use

B.C. Luke

From Seed to Harvest: Cannabis Edition

1.
2.
3.
4.
5.
6.
7.
8.
9.
10.
11.
12.

Chapter One

Introduction to Cannabis Cultivation

Cultivating cannabis opens up a world of both ancient traditions and modern innovations. The journey begins with understanding the rich history of this versatile plant, stretching back thousands of years across various cultures. From its early uses for fibers and medicinal purposes to its integration into spiritual practices, cannabis has left an indelible mark on human history. This chapter will take you through that historical tapestry, showcasing how different civilizations utilized and valued cannabis.

As we progress, you'll dive into the basics of home growing, starting with the undeniable benefits it offers in quality control and cost savings. We'll clear up common misconceptions and shine a light on the necessary tools and techniques that can turn any hobbyist gardener into a successful cannabis grower. Legal considerations are also crucial, and this chapter will guide you through the complexities of local regulations to ensure your cultivation efforts remain compliant and thriving. By the end, you'll appreciate not just how to cultivate cannabis but why it's an endeavor worth undertaking.

History and Evolution of Cannabis Cultivation

Cannabis cultivation has a rich and diverse history that spans thousands of years, with its roots deeply entrenched in various cultures around the globe. The historical journey of cannabis is fascinating and offers valuable insights into its uses and evolution.

Ancient origins of cannabis can be traced back to ancient civilizations where it was primarily cultivated for its fibers, seeds, and medicinal properties. The oldest known written record on cannabis use comes from the Chinese Emperor Shen Nung in 2727 B.C. This illustrates how far back the knowledge and utilization of cannabis extend. In Egypt, it was used as a remedy for sore eyes and cataract treatments. Ancient Greeks and Romans were also familiar with cannabis, utilizing its seeds for nutrition and oil production. In the Middle East, the use of cannabis spread throughout the Islamic empire to North Africa, where it was employed for various medicinal purposes.

The evolution of cannabis cultivation over time showcases the adaptability and versatility of this plant. From ancient agricultural practices, where it was grown alongside other essential crops, to more sophisticated modern-day techniques, cannabis cultivation has seen significant advancement. Historically, cannabis was grown in large fields and harvested manually, but today's growers often use hydroponic systems, advanced lighting, and climate control technologies to optimize yield and potency. This shift reflects a broader trend towards more efficient and specialized cultivation methods, acknowledging the growing demand for both recreational and medicinal cannabis.

Legislation changes have played a crucial role in shaping the cultivation and perception of cannabis throughout history. In many regions, cannabis transitioned from being a widely accepted plant for various uses to becoming a controlled substance due to shifting political and social climates. For instance, in the early 20th century, racial and political factors in the United States led to the criminalization of marijuana through laws such as the Marijuana Tax Act of 1937. This act imposed heavy restrictions on the cultivation and distribution of cannabis. However, in present times, many places are witnessing a resurgence in legalization efforts for both medical and recreational use. Understanding these legal shifts helps readers navigate current laws and appreciate the evolving dialogue surrounding cannabis cultivation.

The global spread of cannabis cultivation highlights the plant's remarkable ability to adapt to different environments and cultural contexts. Cannabis originally evolved in Central Asia before spreading to Africa, Europe, and eventually the Americas. In North America, early colonists grew hemp for textiles and rope, recognizing its value as a fast-growing and versatile crop. Spanish settlers introduced cannabis to South America in the 16th century, where it became integrated into local agricultural practices. Over time, various regions developed unique growing styles and traditions tailored to their specific climates and needs.

In the African continent, cannabis was introduced by Arab traders and quickly became an integral part of traditional medicine and cultural rituals. Countries like Morocco became renowned for their high-quality hashish production, which involved specific cultivation and processing techniques. In India, cannabis has been intertwined with religious practices for centuries, particularly within Hindu and Sikh communities, where it is consumed during ceremonies and festivals.

As cannabis cultivation spread globally, it also led to the development of diverse strains and varieties. These strains were adapted to various climates and purposes, ranging from industrial hemp to psychoactive marijuana. The global exchange of cannabis genetics further enriched the cultivation practices, allowing for innovations such as crossbreeding and hybridization to create strains with desired traits. This adaptability underscores the plant's historical significance and ongoing relevance in modern agriculture.

Reflecting on the ancient origins and evolution of cannabis cultivation provides context for understanding the current state of cannabis cultivation. Lessons from historical practices can inform modern growers about sustainable and effective techniques. For example, ancient methods of companion planting—where cannabis was grown alongside other crops to benefit from natural pest control and soil enrichment—can inspire contemporary organic farming practices.

Recognizing the cultural significance of cannabis adds another layer of appreciation to its cultivation. In various cultures, cannabis was not merely a plant but a symbol of resilience, spirituality, and communal identity. From the sacred rituals of shamans in ancient Siberia who used burnt cannabis seeds to connect with the spiritual realm, to the Rastafarian movement in Jamaica that regards cannabis as a sacramental herb, the plant has held profound meaning across time and space.

Moreover, awareness of the changing perceptions and legal landscapes informs responsible cultivation practices today. As more regions move towards legalization, it is imperative for growers to stay informed about local regulations and best practices to ensure compliance and quality. Historical context helps in understanding the ongoing debates regarding cannabis and appreciating the progress made towards its acceptance and normalization.

Benefits, Tools, and Legal Considerations of Home Growing

Exploring the myriad benefits of cultivating cannabis at home, one quickly realizes the unique advantages in quality control, cost savings, and the satisfaction that comes from personal involvement in the growing process. By growing cannabis at home, individuals have complete oversight on every aspect of their cultivation, leading to a higher quality product. They can choose organic nutrients, avoid harmful pesticides, and harvest the plants at their peak potency. This level of control ensures that the end product is not only safe but tailored to specific needs, whether for medical or recreational use.

Cost savings represent another significant benefit of home cannabis cultivation. While the initial setup might require some investment in tools and equipment, these costs are often offset over time. For instance, by reusing seeds and clones, growers can substantially reduce expenses. Moreover, eliminating the need for packaging and transportation contributes to further savings. In areas where cannabis products are heavily taxed, home growing bypasses the additional financial burden, providing economic relief for regular users.

To embark on this journey of home cultivation, understanding the necessary tools and equipment is crucial. The foundation of any successful grow operation starts with choosing the right growing medium. Options range from traditional soil to hydroponic and aeroponic systems, each offering different benefits and complexities. Soil is user-friendly and familiar to many hobbyist gardeners, while hydroponics can provide faster growth and greater yield by directly delivering nutrients to the roots.

Lighting systems are paramount as well, particularly for indoor grows. High-Intensity Discharge (HID) lights, such as Metal Halide (MH) and High-Pressure Sodium (HPS), have long been used due to their effectiveness. However, advancements in technology have made Light Emitting Diodes (LEDs) a popular choice for their energy efficiency and ability to provide full-spectrum lighting tailored to different stages of plant growth.

Environmental control tools are essential to mimic the ideal conditions for cannabis growth. This includes maintaining proper temperature, humidity, and ventilation. Fans, dehumidifiers, and air conditioning units help regulate the climate within the grow space, ensuring that plants flourish. Additionally, pH meters and nutrient testing kits are indispensable for monitoring the health of the plants and making necessary adjustments.

The legal considerations of home cannabis cultivation cannot be overlooked. Laws surrounding cannabis cultivation vary significantly from one region to another, making it imperative to understand and comply with local regulations. In areas where cannabis cultivation is legal, there are typically strict guidelines regarding the number of plants allowed per household, the location of the grow operation, and security measures to prevent unauthorized access.

In many regions, medicinal cannabis patients may have more lenient regulations allowing them to grow more plants than recreational users, provided they have a valid prescription. For instance, some jurisdictions permit registered medical marijuana patients to cultivate up to six mature plants, while recreational users might be limited to four. It is also common for laws to stipulate that cannabis plants must be kept out of public view and secured to prevent theft or access by minors.

Understanding the legal landscape is crucial not only to avoid potential legal repercussions but also to ensure a respectful coexistence with neighbors and the community. Engaging with local authorities or consulting legal experts can provide clarity and peace of mind, enabling home growers to focus on cultivating high-quality cannabis without fear of violating the law.

Growing cannabis at home offers numerous personal benefits beyond quality control and cost savings. The hands-on experience nurtures a deeper connection with the plant and heightens appreciation for the art of cultivation. Each phase—from selecting seeds or clones to witnessing the germination, vegetative growth, flowering, and finally, harvesting—brings its own set of rewards and learning opportunities.

For medical cannabis patients, the ability to grow specific strains tailored to their conditions provides therapeutic benefits that might not be readily available through commercial channels. Cultivating strains with precise levels of cannabinoids like CBD (Cannabidiol) and THC (Tetrahydrocannabinol) allows patients to manage symptoms effectively and safely. Furthermore, knowing exactly what goes into the growing process reassures patients about the purity and safety of their medicine.

Recreational users also stand to benefit from the customization afforded by home cultivation. Experimenting with different strains, growing techniques, and harvest times enables users to produce cannabis that meets their preferences, whether that means maximizing potency, enhancing flavor profiles, or balancing the effects of different cannabinoids and terpenes.

The social aspect of cannabis cultivation should not be underestimated either. Home growers often find camaraderie and support within gardening communities, both locally and online. Sharing tips, discussing challenges, and celebrating successes can make the cultivation journey even more fulfilling. Whether it's comparing notes on the best nutrients or trading seeds to diversify one's garden, the collective knowledge and encouragement found in these communities enhance the growing experience.

While the initial steps into home cannabis cultivation might seem daunting, the wealth of resources available today makes it accessible to anyone willing to invest the time and effort. Books, online forums, instructional videos, and workshops offer valuable information to guide new growers through every stage of the process. Moreover, local hydroponic stores and gardening centers frequently provide expert advice tailored to the regional climate and growing conditions.

Final Insights

In this chapter, we've journeyed through the rich history and evolution of cannabis cultivation. We've explored how ancient civilizations used the plant for various purposes, from medicinal remedies to fibers and seeds. We also looked at how cultivation techniques have advanced over time, moving from simple agricultural practices to modern methods using sophisticated technology. Recognizing the cultural significance and historical context of cannabis helps us appreciate not just its past but also its ongoing relevance in today's world.

We've also delved into the many benefits of home growing, such as quality control and cost savings. By understanding the necessary tools and equipment, hobbyist gardeners and patients alike can successfully cultivate their cannabis plants at home. It's important to stay informed about the ever-changing legal landscape to ensure responsible growing practices. Whether you're looking to enhance your gardening skills, manage medical conditions, or simply explore the rewarding process of growing your own cannabis, this chapter provides a solid foundation to get you started on your journey.

Reference List

Admin, T. J. (2024, June 14). *Homegrown Weed vs Dispensary - Which Is Right for You?* The Joint LLC. https://thejointllc.com/homegrown-weed-vs-dispensary/

Cannabis . (2021). Museum.dea.gov. https://museum.dea.gov/exhibits/online-exhibits/cannabis-coca-and-poppy-natures-addictive-plants/cannabis

Grow Your Own Cannabis at Home: The Benefits and How-To Guide | 2024 □□ . (2023, June 11). Seedsherenow.com. https://seedsherenow.com/grow-your-own-cannabis-at-home-the-benefits-and-how-to-guide/

History.com Editors. (2017, May 31). *Marijuana* . HISTORY; A&E Television Networks. https://www.history.com/topics/crime/history-of-marijuana

Chapter Two

Understanding Cannabis Biology and Genetics

Understanding the biology and genetics of cannabis plants is key to successful cultivation. With a rich history that spans centuries, cannabis has evolved in complexity, making it essential for growers to grasp its fundamental biological structures and genetic makeup. This understanding not only aids in proper plant care but also paves the way for achieving desired effects, whether for medicinal, recreational, or wellness purposes.

In this chapter, we delve into the intricate details of cannabis plant anatomy, starting from the roots and moving upwards through the stems, branches, leaves, and flowers. You will learn about the critical roles each part plays in the plant's overall health and productivity. We will explore how to monitor root health, optimize nutrient uptake, and employ effective pruning techniques. Additionally, the differences between indica, sativa, and hybrid strains will be discussed, providing insights into their unique growth patterns and effects. By the end of this chapter, you'll have a comprehensive understanding of cannabis biology and genetics, equipping you with the knowledge to enhance your cultivation skills and achieve optimal results.

Cannabis Plant Anatomy

Understanding the various parts of the cannabis plant and their distinct functions is essential for successful cultivation. This knowledge helps growers create optimal conditions for the plant's development, leading to healthier growth and higher yields.

Starting from the bottom, roots play a crucial role in supporting the cannabis plant. They anchor the plant in the soil, ensuring stability and preventing it from toppling over. The root system, comprised of a primary taproot and branching fibrous roots, penetrates deep into the soil to absorb water and nutrients, which are vital for the plant's growth. Strong root networks relate directly to efficient nutrient uptake, making nutrient solutions accessible throughout the plant's life cycle. To monitor the health of the roots, growers should look out for white, firm roots. Rotting or discolored roots can indicate poor health and might point to problems like overwatering, poor soil drainage, or disease (Andrews, 2024). Understanding root health and addressing any issues proactively can prevent significant growth problems down the line. For example, incorporating supplements like Indolebutyric Acid (IBA) can promote better rooting, enhancing overall plant vigor (Marijuana Plant Anatomy, n.d.).

Moving upward, the stems and branches of the cannabis plant provide critical support and facilitate nutrient transport. The stem serves as the central backbone, holding up leaves and flowers while distributing nutrients absorbed by the roots. Within the stem, vascular bundles transport water, minerals, and nutrients to different parts of the plant – the xylem moves water and minerals upwards, and the phloem distributes sugars and other metabolic products (Andrews, 2024). Proper pruning and training practices such as topping and low-stress training (LST) enhance branch development. These methods encourage the plant to grow more bud sites, ultimately increasing yield. Recognizing signals from the stems about their health can offer insights into the plant's overall well-being. For instance, a robust, thick stem indicates healthy development, whereas a thin, weak stem might suggest underlying issues that need to be addressed.

Leaves are the solar panels of the cannabis plant, indispensable for photosynthesis. Photosynthesis is the process through which plants convert sunlight into energy, using chlorophyll to capture light. Healthy leaves are green, sturdy, and fully formed. Any deviations, such as yellowing or curling, can indicate nutrient deficiencies or pest infestations. Leaves also exhibit early warning signs if something is amiss; for example, a nitrogen deficiency often manifests as yellowing leaves at the bottom of the plant, while calcium deficiency might show as brown or burned spots on leaf edges. Regular monitoring and immediate corrective measures, such as adjusting nutrient levels or improving lighting conditions, can help maintain robust foliage and ensure effective photosynthesis.

The flowers of the cannabis plant are not only its reproductive organs but also the primary source of cannabinoids, which are compounds responsible for the therapeutic effects of cannabis. Female flowers, or buds, are what growers usually aim to harvest as they contain the highest concentrations of cannabinoids like THC and CBD. Male plants produce pollen sacs rather than buds and are typically removed from the garden to prevent pollination, which leads to seed production in female plants and reduces the quality and potency of the buds. Identifying the sex of your plants early on is crucial – female plants will develop pistils (hair-like structures), while males will form round pollen sacs at the nodes (points where leaves attach to the stem).

Proper care during the flowering stage is pivotal to maximize the potency and quality of the final product. This phase requires particular attention to environmental conditions such as light, humidity, and temperature. A consistent light schedule, adequate airflow, and controlled humidity levels help prevent mold and mildew, especially since the resin-rich trichomes on buds can attract moisture. Trichomes, the tiny glandular hairs covering the buds, produce the aromatic oils and cannabinoids that give cannabis its distinctive properties. These structures also serve as protective barriers against pests and environmental stressors.

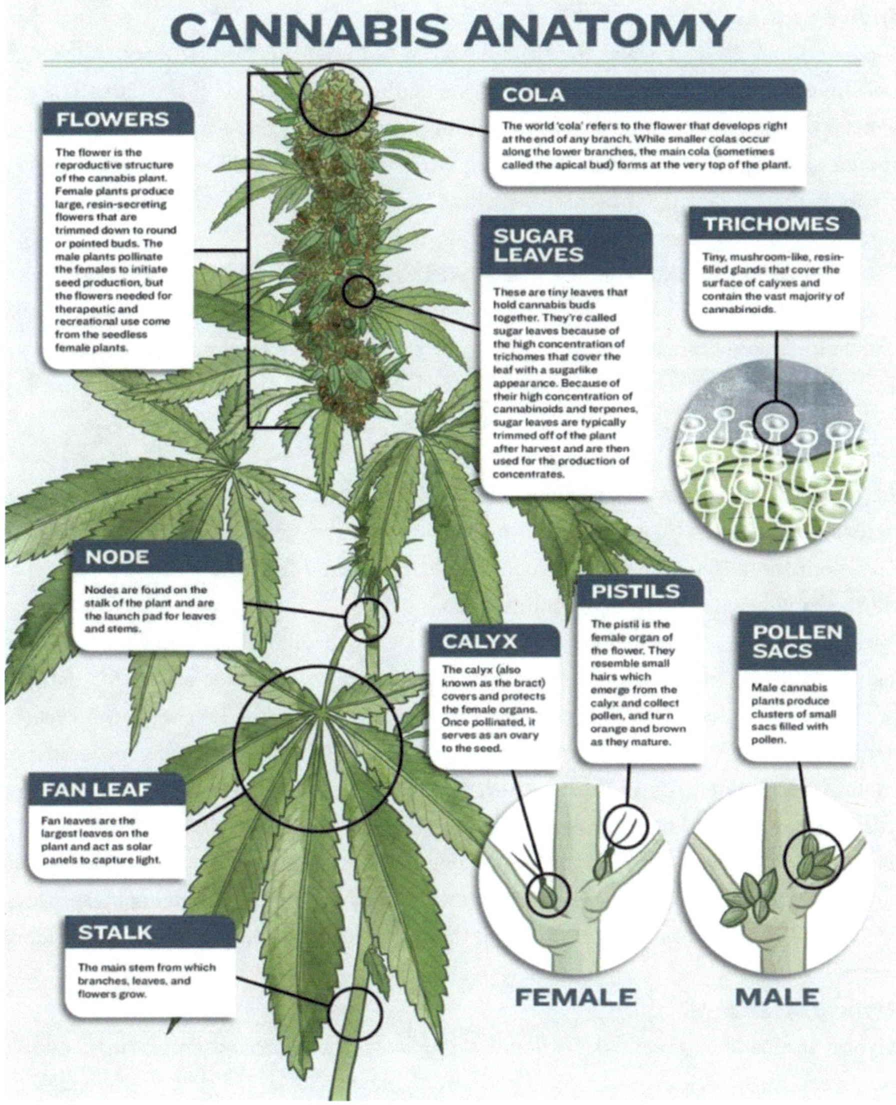

Indica vs. Sativa vs. Hybrid Strains

Understanding Cannabis Biology and Genetics

When delving into the world of cannabis cultivation, understanding the distinct characteristics of different cannabis strains is paramount. This foundational knowledge will help hobbyist gardeners, medical cannabis patients, caregivers, and recreational users make informed decisions that suit their specific needs and preferences.

Indica Strains

Indica strains are renowned for their deeply relaxing effects, which many users find beneficial for unwinding, stress relief, and aiding sleep. These plants are typically shorter and bushier than their sativa counterparts, making them more manageable in indoor growing environments. Their compact structure allows them to produce higher yields within a shorter growth cycle. This characteristic is particularly appealing for those with limited space or the desire for quicker harvests.

The physical attributes of indica plants, such as their broad leaves and dense buds, contribute to their resilience in varied conditions. This resilience makes them a solid choice for beginners who might still be mastering the nuances of cannabis cultivation. By thriving in smaller spaces and under artificial lighting, indica strains offer versatility for those looking to grow indoors all year round.

Sativa Strains

In contrast, sativa strains are famed for their uplifting and energizing effects, often described as a "mind high." They are ideal for daytime use, providing a burst of creativity and motivation. However, these benefits come with certain cultivation requirements that differ significantly from those of indica strains.

Sativa plants are generally taller and have thinner, finger-like leaves. They require more light and space to reach their full potential, making them better suited for outdoor growing conditions where they can bask in natural sunlight. The longer growth cycle of sativa strains means that growers need to be patient, as these plants take more time to mature compared to indicas. However, this patience is often rewarded with robust plants and abundant, high-quality yields.

For those with ample outdoor space and favorable climate conditions, sativas can be an excellent choice. Their ability to grow tall and thrive in open environments makes them a favorite for gardeners looking to expand their cultivation beyond the confines of indoor setups.

Hybrid Strains

Hybrid strains offer a blend of both indica and sativa characteristics, providing a middle ground that combines desirable traits from each. These hybrids are created by crossbreeding various parent plants to achieve specific effects and growth patterns. As a result, hybrid strains can cater to a wide range of user preferences and cultivation conditions.

One of the main advantages of hybrid strains is their versatility. Whether you're looking for a balanced effect that includes both relaxation and mental stimulation, or you have unique growing constraints, there is likely a hybrid strain suited to your needs. For instance, some hybrids are bred specifically to flourish in both indoor and outdoor environments, offering flexibility for growers regardless of their setup.

Hybrids also provide an opportunity for growers to experiment and find the perfect strain that meets their personal requirements. By understanding the dominant characteristics of the parent strains used to create a hybrid, cultivators can predict and influence the outcome, tailoring their growing strategies to optimize results.

Choosing the Right Strain

Selecting the appropriate cannabis strain involves careful consideration of several factors: the intended effects, the growing conditions available, and individual preferences. For hobbyist gardeners, the primary goal may be to successfully grow healthy plants with minimal fuss. In this case, choosing strains known for their resilience and ease of cultivation, such as certain indicas or well-balanced hybrids, can lead to satisfying and productive gardening experiences.

Medical cannabis patients and caregivers must prioritize specific therapeutic effects when selecting strains. For instance, patients seeking pain relief or help with insomnia might prefer indica-dominant strains due to their sedative properties. Conversely, those needing daytime symptom management, such as increased energy or mood enhancement, might lean towards sativa-dominant strains.

For recreational users, the focus might be on finding strains that align with social activities or personal relaxation routines. Here, hybrids can be particularly valuable, offering a variety of tailored experiences. By experimenting with different hybrids, users can discover what works best for their lifestyle and wellness goals.

It's also essential to consider the growing environment when choosing a strain. Indoor growers should assess their space limitations, light availability, and temperature control capabilities. Meanwhile, outdoor growers must account for regional climate, natural light cycles, and potential pests. Selecting strains that align with these environmental factors can greatly enhance the success and satisfaction of the cultivation process.

Guidelines for Optimal Cultivation

To optimize growth and achieve the desired effects, it's important to follow some basic guidelines tailored to each type of strain:

1. **Indica Strains:** Ensure adequate ventilation and manage humidity levels to prevent mold, which can thrive in the dense foliage typical of indica plants. Regular pruning can help maintain airflow and light penetration, promoting healthier growth and higher yields.

1. **Sativa Strains:** Provide ample vertical space and robust support structures for the tall, lanky growth habit of sativa plants. Given their longer growth cycle, consistent nutrient management is crucial to sustain vigorous growth over extended periods.

1. **Hybrid Strains:** Monitor and adjust growing techniques based on the dominant traits of the hybrid strain. For example, if the hybrid leans towards indica characteristics, indoor pruning and height management may be necessary. Conversely, if sativa traits dominate, ensure sufficient light and vertical space.
1. **Environmental Considerations:** Tailor the growing environment to match the strain's needs. Indicas often perform well in controlled indoor settings, while sativas benefit from the expansive conditions provided by outdoor gardens. Hybrids may have more diverse requirements but often adapt well to various conditions with proper care.

By taking the time to understand and implement these guidelines, growers can maximize the potential of their chosen cannabis strains, resulting in healthier plants and more rewarding harvests. This thoughtful approach not only enhances the quality of the cultivated product but also enriches the overall experience of growing cannabis.

Summary and Reflections

Understanding the intricate details of cannabis plant anatomy is key to successful cultivation. From hardy roots that secure and nourish, to sturdy stems and branches that support growth, every part of the plant plays a vital role. Leaves act as energy factories through photosynthesis, while healthy flowers promise rich cannabinoid content. By paying attention to these aspects and ensuring each part gets what it needs, cultivators can anticipate more robust and fruitful plants.

As growers become familiar with the unique characteristics of their plants, they can address issues early, adjust growing conditions, and ultimately maximize yields. This foundational knowledge sets the stage for experimenting with different strains and enhancing overall gardening skills. Whether you're a hobbyist, medical patient, or simply curious about cannabis, mastering plant anatomy will undoubtedly improve your growing experience and lead to a bountiful harvest.

Reference List

Andrews, E. (2024, March 13). *Anatomy of the Cannabis Plant: Exploring its Parts* . Curio Wellness™. https://curiowellness.com/blog/anatomy-of-the-cannabis-plant/

Contributors, W. E. (n.d.). *Indica vs. Sativa: What's the Difference?* WebMD. https://www.webmd.com/mental-health/addiction/indica-vs-sativa-whats-the-difference

Holland, K. (2019, April 8). *Sativa vs. Indica: What to Expect Across Cannabis Types and Strains* . Healthline; Healthline Media. https://www.healthline.com/health/sativa-vs-indica

Marijuana Plant Anatomy . (n.d.). Leafly.
https://www.leafly.com/learn/growing/marijuana-plant-anatomy

Chapter Three

Seed Selection and Germination

Selecting top-quality cannabis seeds and kick-starting the germination process are the heartbeats of successful cannabis cultivation. Whether you are an enthusiastic home gardener, a medical marijuana patient, or someone exploring cannabis for personal wellness, understanding these initial steps can greatly influence your plant's performance and yield. The intricacies of seed selection and germination are often overlooked but are essential for achieving healthy, robust plants that thrive under various growing conditions. By giving proper attention to these foundational steps, you'll set the stage for a fruitful gardening experience.

In this chapter, we will delve into the nuances of choosing the best seeds for your specific needs, considering factors like seed type, size, color, and origin. We'll explore different categories of seeds such as regular, feminized, and autoflower, each offering unique advantages depending on your cultivation goals and environment. Following seed selection, we'll walk through various germination methods, detailing their pros and cons to help you find the most effective technique for your grow setup. From the paper towel method to direct soil planting, you'll gain insights into creating optimal conditions for your seeds to sprout and flourish. Embark on this journey with us to master the art of seed selection and germination, ensuring a strong start to your cannabis growing venture.

Types of Cannabis Seeds (Regular, Feminized, Autoflower)

Let's dive right in!

Understanding the variety of cannabis seeds available is crucial for hobbyist gardeners, medical cannabis patients, and recreational users aiming to optimize their cultivation process. The type of seed chosen can significantly impact the growth cycle, yield, and overall health of your cannabis plants. Here's a breakdown of the different types of cannabis seeds and how they influence your gardening experience.

Regular Seeds

Regular seeds are the natural result produced by male and female cannabis plant pollination. These seeds have a roughly equal chance of developing into male or female plants. For growers interested in breeding new strains, regular seeds provide an opportunity to maintain genetic diversity and create unique hybrids. However, one challenge with regular seeds is the need to identify and remove male plants early in the flowering stage. Failure to do this could result in unwanted pollination, leading to seed production instead of bud formation.

For example, identifying male plants usually involves looking for pollen sacs, whereas female plants develop pistils. This process requires careful monitoring and some level of experience, which can be daunting for novice growers. Despite these challenges, regular seeds offer the benefit of robust genetic vigor, making them a favorite among traditionalists and breeders who appreciate the variability and potential for creating something unique.

Feminized Seeds

Feminized seeds are engineered to produce only female plants, which are the ones that generate the most valuable parts of the cannabis plant — the buds. This type of seed simplifies the growing process by eliminating the need to weed out male plants, thereby maximizing flower production. This makes feminized seeds particularly appealing to beginners who want to focus on increasing their yields without worrying about sexing the plants.

The creation of feminized seeds involves stressing female plants to produce pollen, which is then used to fertilize other female plants. The result is seeds that carry only female chromosomes. While this process sounds complex, it translates into a simpler growing experience for you. This is especially beneficial for those aiming for high yields and quality flowers, as all your plants will contribute to the harvest. Feminized seeds are a great choice for both hobbyist gardeners and those growing cannabis for medical purposes, where the focus is on harvesting abundant and potent buds.

Autoflower Seeds

Autoflower seeds represent a significant advancement in cannabis cultivation technology. Unlike regular and feminized seeds, autoflower seeds transition from the vegetative stage to the flowering phase based on their age, rather than changes in the light cycle. This characteristic stems from their genetic heritage, often incorporating Cannabis Ruderalis, a subspecies known for its ability to flower automatically in response to age rather than light conditions.

This trait makes autoflower seeds ideal for those seeking multiple harvests within a single growing season. Autoflowers generally have shorter life cycles, meaning you can achieve several harvests per year. Their smaller stature and faster maturation make them perfect for growers with limited space or those wanting quick results. However, it's worth noting that the shorter lifecycle can sometimes mean slightly lower yields compared to photoperiod strains. But the trade-off is balanced by the ability to harvest more frequently, making autoflower seeds a favorite among novice growers and those with limited time.

Choosing the Right Type

Choosing the right type of cannabis seed depends largely on your growing conditions, goals, and local climate. If you're working with a limited indoor growing space, feminized or autoflower seeds might be your best bet due to their predictable outcomes and ease of management. However, if you have a larger outdoor area and an interest in breeding, regular seeds could offer you the flexibility and genetic diversity you're after.

Consider your end goals: Are you growing for personal enjoyment, medicinal use, or even venture into small-scale commercial cultivation? Feminized seeds are excellent for maximizing yield and potency, making them suitable for medicinal growers who need consistent and reliable results. On the other hand, regular seeds offer genetic robustness, essential for anyone looking to experiment with crossbreeding or preserving rare genetics.

Climate also plays a vital role in your decision. Autoflower seeds perform exceptionally well in diverse climates due to their resilience and shorter growing periods. They can complete their cycle before harsher weather sets in, making them ideal for regions with shorter summers. In contrast, regular and feminized seeds might require more controlled environments, especially in areas prone to extreme weather.

Economic factors shouldn't be overlooked either. While feminized and autoflower seeds might come at a premium price given their specialized breeding processes, they often result in higher yields and fewer wasted resources. Investing in these seeds can be more cost-effective in the long run, especially when considering the time and effort saved in not having to identify and eliminate male plants.

Each type of seed offers distinct advantages tailored to different growing environments and goals. By understanding these options and aligning them with your specific needs, you can substantially enhance your cannabis cultivation journey. Selecting the right seed type forms the foundation of a successful harvest, ensuring your efforts translate into a bountiful return.

Evaluating Seed Quality and Germination Methods

Identifying high-quality cannabis seeds is the first critical step in ensuring a bountiful harvest. Healthy seeds possess distinct physical traits such as color, size, and surface texture. Typically, robust seeds are dark brown or even black, with a slight sheen indicating their vitality. In contrast, seeds that appear white or green are often immature and less likely to germinate successfully. Size can also be an indicator; plump, larger seeds tend to be healthier, while smaller seeds might not contain sufficient nutrients to sustain germination. Additionally, a smooth, unblemished surface without cracks or dents suggests resilience and durability.

The origin of your cannabis seeds plays a pivotal role in determining their quality. Sourcing seeds from reputable breeders or established seed banks is paramount. These providers often have stringent quality control measures and breeding programs to ensure that their seeds carry good genetics. When purchasing seeds, it's a good idea to read reviews and testimonials from other growers. This feedback can offer insights into the breeder's reputation and the performance of their seeds under real-world conditions. Avoid seeds from undefined or dubious sources, such as those found in low-quality cannabis buds, as these are often of inferior quality and questionable genetic lineage.

Once you've selected your seeds, the germination process begins, and there are several methods to consider. The paper towel method is one of the most popular techniques among growers due to its simplicity and effectiveness. To start, dampen two paper towels with water, being careful not to oversaturate them. Place one of the moist paper towels on a plate, then spread the seeds across it, ensuring they're spaced apart to prevent roots from tangling. Cover the seeds with the second damp paper towel and place another plate on top to create a humid environment. Store this setup in a warm, dark location, ideally between 70-85 degrees Fahrenheit (21-29°C). Check the paper towels regularly to maintain moisture levels, and within 24 to 72 hours, you should see the seeds begin to crack open, revealing tiny roots. At this stage, the germinating seeds can be carefully transplanted into soil or another growing medium.

Alternatively, the direct soil method can be used for germination. This approach mimics natural conditions and reduces handling stress on young seedlings, which can sometimes lead to transplant shock. Begin by filling small pots or seedling trays with high-quality seedling soil or a light potting mix. Ensure the soil is loose, well-draining, and nutrient-rich to support early growth. Make a small hole about a quarter-inch deep using a trowel or your finger, and place the seed in the hole with the pointed end facing down. Cover the seed lightly with soil and gently moisten it with water. The key here is to keep the soil damp but not waterlogged, as excess moisture can cause the seeds to rot. Placing the pots in a warm, dark environment will help maintain the ideal temperature range of 70-85 degrees Fahrenheit (21-29°C). Within a few days to a week, the seedlings should emerge, at which point they need to be moved to a location with ample light.

When choosing between these germination methods, consider the specific needs and constraints of your growing environment. The paper towel method allows for close monitoring and faster results in some cases, but it requires careful handling when transferring the delicate seedlings to soil. On the other hand, the direct soil method is more hands-off and better simulates natural growing conditions, which can be beneficial for minimizing stress on the plants.

Bringing It All Together

In this chapter, we've explored the different types of cannabis seeds—regular, feminized, and autoflower—and how each plays a unique role in the growing process. By understanding their distinct characteristics and benefits, you can make informed decisions that align with your cultivation goals, whether you're aiming for genetic diversity, high yields, or multiple harvests within a season. This knowledge equips you to choose seeds that will thrive in your specific growing environment, whether indoors, outdoors, or in variable climates.

We've also delved into evaluating seed quality and germination methods, emphasizing the importance of selecting robust seeds from reputable sources. With techniques like the paper towel method and direct soil planting, you're now equipped to kickstart your cannabis growing journey effectively. Remember, successful cultivation begins with the right seeds and proper germination practices, setting a solid foundation for a rewarding and fruitful harvest. Happy growing!

Reference List

A Guide to Marijuana Seed Selection . (n.d.). Sites.utexas.edu. https://sites.utexas.edu/discovery/2023/11/06/a-guide-to-marijuana-seed-selection/

How can you tell if your Cannabis Seeds Are Good - Ed Rosenthal and Royal Queen Seeds . (2021, February 22). Ed Rosenthal. https://www.edrosenthal.com/the-guru-of-ganja-blog/2021/2/22/how-to-tell-if-your-cannabis-seeds-are-good

How To Identify High-Quality Cannabis Seeds: A Simple Guide . (2024, June 7). Seedsherenow.com. https://seedsherenow.com/how-to-identify-high-quality-cannabis-seeds/

Understanding Cannabis Seed Categories: Key Types | 2024 . (2024, February 20). Seedsherenow.com. https://seedsherenow.com/cannabis-seed-categories/

Chapter Four

Indoor Growing Setup

Setting up the perfect indoor growing environment for cannabis starts with choosing the right grow lights and understanding how light cycles affect plant development. The type of light you use can have a major impact on everything from plant health to yield, making it one of the most crucial decisions you'll make in your indoor gardening journey. With various options available like LED, HPS, and CFL lights, each offering its unique benefits and drawbacks, selecting the optimal lighting setup is key to a successful grow operation. Just as important is mastering the timing and duration of light exposure—known as light cycles—which are vital for the different growth stages of your cannabis plants.

In this chapter, we'll explore the ins and outs of grow lights, diving into the specifics of LED, HPS, and CFL options to help you understand their advantages and limitations. We'll break down how each type of light affects your plants and what considerations you should keep in mind when setting up your growing space. Additionally, we'll guide you through the essential concept of light cycles, explaining how to implement and manage these cycles effectively to promote healthy growth and abundant yields. By the end of this chapter, you'll be equipped with the knowledge needed to create an ideal lighting environment for your cannabis plants, ensuring they thrive from seedling to harvest.

Choosing the Right Grow Lights and Light Cycles

When starting with an indoor growing setup, particularly for cannabis, one of the most crucial decisions is choosing the right type of grow lights. The type of light you use can significantly impact the health, growth rate, and yield of your plants. Let's dive into the different grow light options available and understand the importance of light cycles for various growth stages.

Firstly, LED grow lights are a favorite among many indoor growers for several reasons. These lights are highly energy-efficient, consuming less power compared to other types of grow lights. This efficiency translates into lower electricity bills, which is always a plus. Moreover, LEDs have a long lifespan, often lasting for many years without needing replacement. One of the standout features of LED grow lights is their ability to be tuned to specific light spectrums. Different stages of plant growth, such as vegetative and flowering stages, require different light spectrums. With LEDs, you can easily adjust the spectrum to provide your plants with the ideal light conditions they need at each growth stage. For instance, during the vegetative stage, plants benefit from blue light, which promotes leafy growth. During the flowering stage, red light helps stimulate bud production.

On the other hand, HPS (High-Pressure Sodium) lights have been a staple in the world of indoor growing for decades. They produce a strong light output that is highly effective for both the flowering and vegetative stages of cannabis growth. However, there are some considerations to keep in mind when using HPS lights. They generate a significant amount of heat, which means you'll need to implement additional ventilation to prevent your grow space from becoming too hot. Excessive heat can stress your plants, leading to slow growth or even damage. Therefore, investing in good ventilation systems, such as inline fans or exhaust setups, becomes necessary when using HPS lights. Despite this extra requirement, many growers still prefer HPS lights due to their ability to produce high yields and robust plants.

For beginners or those working with smaller grow spaces, CFL (Compact Fluorescent Lamp) lights could be a suitable choice. CFLs are relatively inexpensive compared to other grow lights, making them accessible for those new to indoor growing. Additionally, their compact size and low heat output allow for easier placement within small grow areas. You can position these lights close to your plants without worrying about heat damage, ensuring optimal light coverage. While CFLs might not deliver the same intensity or efficiency as LEDs or HPS lights, they offer a straightforward and cost-effective solution for hobbyist gardeners or small-scale grows.

Now, no matter which type of grow light you choose, understanding and implementing proper light cycles is essential for the successful cultivation of cannabis. Light cycles refer to the duration and timing of light exposure that plants receive during different growth stages. For the vegetative stage, a common light cycle is 18 hours of light followed by six hours of darkness (18/6). This extended period of light encourages vigorous vegetative growth, allowing your plants to develop a strong structure and healthy leaves.

When transitioning to the flowering stage, adjusting the light cycle is critical. A typical light cycle for flowering is 12 hours of light followed by 12 hours of darkness (12/12). The shift to equal periods of light and darkness signals to the plants that it's time to start flowering and producing buds. Consistency in these light schedules is paramount; any disruptions or fluctuations can stress the plants and potentially hinder their development. Using timers can help maintain precise light cycles and ensure your plants receive the correct amount of light at each stage.

Ventilation, Air Circulation, Temperature, and Humidity Control

Creating an optimal indoor grow space for cannabis is key to cultivating healthy plants and achieving maximum yield. Central to this setup is the control of airflow, temperature, and humidity. Properly managing these elements can make a significant difference in plant health, growth rates, and the prevention of issues such as mold.

First, let's talk about airflow. Proper air exchange is crucial because it directly impacts CO2 levels, which plants need for photosynthesis. Without adequate CO2, your plants won't reach their full potential. Additionally, good airflow helps regulate temperature within the grow room. It prevents hot spots from forming near lights or other equipment that generate heat. But perhaps most importantly, proper air exchange reduces the risk of mold and mildew by preventing stagnant, humid air from settling around your plants. Mold spores thrive in stagnant air, especially if it's moist, so this is a step you can't skip.

To achieve proper airflow, consider various fan and exhaust system options. Oscillating fans are great for general air movement; they rotate back and forth to create a breeze that mimics natural wind, strengthening plant stems and promoting better overall growth. Inline fans, on the other hand, are designed to move air through ducting, either bringing fresh air into the grow space or expelling stale air out. Exhaust fans are particularly useful for removing hot, moist air from the room, and many come equipped with carbon filters to help control odor—a feature you might find especially useful if discretion is a concern.

Humidity control is another vital aspect of maintaining a healthy grow environment. Different stages of cannabis growth require varying humidity levels. During the vegetative stage, aim for a relative humidity (RH) of 40-70%. This higher level of moisture supports faster growth and healthier leaves. When your plants enter the flowering stage, reduce the RH to 40-50% to prevent bud rot and other moisture-related issues. Accurate monitoring is essential here, and tools like hygrometers will help you keep track of your room's humidity levels. (*Controlling Humidity Levels in Cannabis Indoor Grow Rooms*, n.d.)

Selecting the right equipment is essential for effective humidity management. Dehumidifiers are invaluable, especially during the flowering stage when lower humidity is required. These devices remove excess moisture from the air, creating a more stable environment. There are two main types: refrigerant-based dehumidifiers, which work well in warmer environments by condensing moisture from the air, and desiccant-based dehumidifiers, which use moisture-absorbing materials and are more energy-efficient, making them suitable for cooler environments. It's important to select a dehumidifier that matches the size of your grow room and its specific humidity control needs. (*Controlling Humidity Levels in Cannabis Indoor Grow Rooms*, n.d.)

Temperature control is equally critical. Cannabis plants have different temperature requirements at various stages of growth. During the vegetative stage, the optimal range is between 70-85°F (21-29°C). This warmth encourages rapid growth and robust foliage development. When plants transition to the flowering stage, slightly lower temperatures of 65-80°F (18-26°C) are ideal, helping to enhance resin production and overall bud quality.

Heaters and air conditioners are your go-to tools for maintaining these temperature ranges. A heater is useful during colder months or nighttime periods when temperatures can drop too low, potentially slowing plant growth or even causing damage. Conversely, air conditioning units can help manage excessive heat, which can stress plants and hinder their development. Investing in reliable heating and cooling systems ensures that your grow room remains within the ideal temperature range, regardless of external weather conditions.

It's also worth noting the benefits of automation in managing these environmental factors. Modern grow rooms often incorporate smart controllers that integrate all aspects of climate control—temperature, humidity, and air flow. These systems allow for precise adjustments and real-time monitoring, making it easier to maintain optimal conditions without constant manual intervention. For instance, an automated system can be set to activate exhaust fans or dehumidifiers whenever humidity exceeds a certain threshold, ensuring that the environment remains conducive to plant health.

Lastly, don't overlook the physical layout of your grow space. Good ventilation requires careful planning of where to place fans and vents. Ensure that fresh air can freely circulate throughout the room and reach all parts of the canopy. Stagnant corners can become breeding grounds for pests and diseases, undermining your efforts to create a healthy environment. Proper sealing and insulation of the grow room also contribute to better climate control. Gaps or leaks can lead to unwanted temperature fluctuations and humidity levels, so make sure to seal any openings with weatherstripping or caulk.

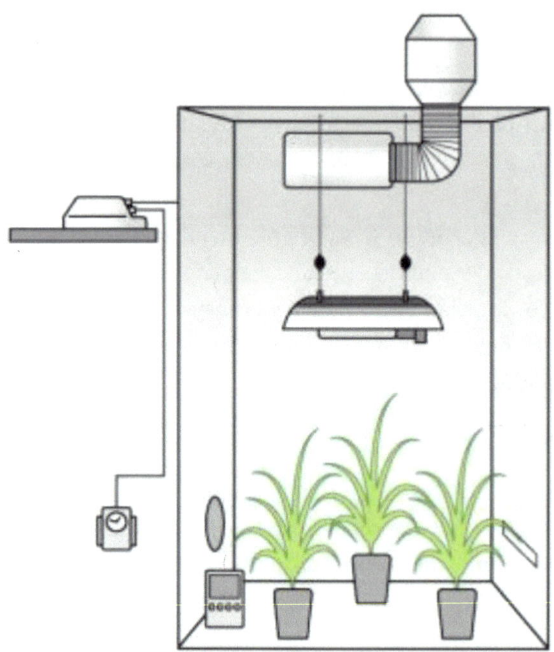

Summary and Reflections

In this chapter, we've explored the essentials of creating an optimal indoor environment for growing cannabis. From selecting the right grow lights to understanding light cycles, you've gained insights into how different types of lights like LEDs, HPS, and CFLs can impact your plant's growth. Remember, matching the light spectrum and light cycle to the specific growth stage is crucial for healthy plants and bountiful yields.

We've also covered vital aspects like airflow, temperature, and humidity control, all necessary for a thriving grow space. Proper ventilation helps maintain CO_2 levels and prevents mold, while managing temperature and humidity ensures your plants can flourish at every stage. With the right tools and setups, you're well on your way to cultivating robust and productive cannabis plants in your indoor garden.

Reference List

Controlling Humidity Levels in Cannabis Indoor Grow Rooms . (n.d.). Floraflex.com. Retrieved August 2, 2024, from https://floraflex.com/UK/blog/post/controlling-humidity-levels-in-cannabis-indoor-grow-rooms

Hasenkopf, E. (2023, October 26). *Mastering Temperature and Humidity Control in Your Indoor Grow Space* . LED Grow Lights Depot. https://www.ledgrowlightsdepot.com/blogs/blog/mastering-temperature-and-humidity-control-in-your-indoor-grow-space

Chapter Five

Outdoor Growing Techniques

Growing cannabis outdoors is all about understanding and working with nature to cultivate healthy, productive plants. The foundation of your success lies in choosing the right site that maximizes sunlight exposure and accessibility, while also considering factors like temperature tolerance and humidity levels. An ideal location ensures your plants receive ample light throughout the day and are protected from extreme weather conditions.

This chapter will guide you through crucial steps such as preparing the soil to ensure it's fertile and well-drained, protecting your plants from pests using both natural and mechanical means, and setting up efficient watering systems. You'll learn how to select a site that not only meets the plants' growing needs but also complies with legal regulations to avoid any potential issues. Whether you're a seasoned gardener or new to cannabis cultivation, these techniques will help you create a thriving outdoor garden.

Selecting an Outdoor Site and Climate Considerations

Choosing the perfect outdoor location for cultivating cannabis is a critical first step that can significantly impact your plants' growth and yield. To optimize your growing site, you must consider factors like sunlight exposure, accessibility, surveillance, temperature tolerance, and humidity levels. Let's delve into each of these aspects.

Sunlight Exposure

Cannabis plants thrive with abundant sunlight, as it fuels photosynthesis, driving their growth and development. Aim to select a location that offers at least 6-8 hours of direct sunlight each day. Southern-facing spots are ideal since they tend to receive the most consistent light throughout the day. However, it's also essential to consider how the sun's path changes with the seasons. In early spring and late fall, shadows from nearby trees or buildings might encroach on your garden area, reducing the total amount of sunlight your plants receive.

Also, be cautious of potential shading that could occur during different times of the day due to taller structures or foliage around the chosen spot. Using tools like a sun chart or even observing the plot over several days can help you make an informed decision. Avoid areas with heavy tree coverage unless the trees can be pruned to minimize shading while still offering some protection against harsh winds.

Accessibility and Surveillance

When it comes to maintenance, ease of access cannot be overstated. You will need to tend to your cannabis plants regularly—watering, pruning, checking for pests, and ensuring they remain healthy. Therefore, proximity to your home or a water source can save you time and effort. Think about the daily routine; a nearby spot allows for quick inspections and easier management, especially if unexpected issues arise.

Surveillance is equally important. While you want easy access, you also want a degree of seclusion. A discreet location away from public view helps protect against theft and vandalism. Opt for places that aren't easily visible from roads, neighbors' properties, or walking paths. If necessary, use barriers like fences or hedges to further obscure the growing area. Additionally, be mindful of any nearby traffic patterns that could expose your plants to pollution or road dust, which can negatively affect their health.

Temperature Tolerance and Humidity Levels

Understanding the local climate's typical temperature range and humidity levels is crucial for selecting a suitable growing site. Cannabis generally thrives between 68°F and 85°F. If your area experiences extreme temperatures outside this range, consider creating microclimates to protect your plants. One way to do this is by planting near natural windbreaks such as large rocks, trellises, or bushes, which can offer shelter from cold winds or intense heat.

Humidity plays a significant role in plant health too. High humidity can increase the risk of mold and mildew, while low humidity might lead to dehydration and stress. For regions with high humidity, ensure good air circulation around your plants. Space them adequately apart and avoid overcrowding. This spacing allows for better airflow, reducing moisture build-up. Conversely, in dry climates, mulching around the base of the plants can help retain soil moisture, and using shade cloths during the hottest part of the day can prevent excessive evaporation and overheating.

Additionally, certain geographical features can influence microclimates. Growing on a slight slope can enhance drainage and reduce flooding risks after heavy rain, key in both humid and temperate zones. Also, consider the natural vegetation in the area; native plants often indicate the site's suitability for growing cannabis.

Legal Compliance

While selecting an ideal spot for your garden, don't overlook the importance of legal compliance. Each region has specific laws and zoning regulations regarding cannabis cultivation. Make sure to research these thoroughly to avoid potential legal disputes. Some areas may have restrictions on the number of plants you can grow, distance requirements from public spaces like schools, parks, or neighboring properties, and even visibility mandates, ensuring your plants aren't easily seen from public areas.

Besides local laws, consider property ownership boundaries. Knowing exactly where your property lines are can help avoid conflicts with neighbors who might not appreciate cannabis being grown adjacent to their land. It's often beneficial to install clear markers or physical barriers to delineate your garden clearly. Being fully informed and compliant ensures you can focus on growing without the looming concern of legal repercussions.

Creating Microclimates for Optimal Growth

Advanced growers often create artificial microclimates to maximize plant health and yield. For instance, raised beds can improve soil drainage and warm up faster than ground soil, benefiting root development in cooler climates. Utilizing fabric pots allows you to move plants to sunnier or more sheltered locations as needed. Similarly, greenhouses or hoop houses extend the growing season by providing protection from extreme weather conditions and allowing for controlled humidity and temperature settings.

Implementing windbreaks like fences, bushes, or even specialized garden netting can shield your plants from strong gusts that could otherwise cause damage. These windbreaks also help maintain a stable temperature around your plants, preventing drastic fluctuations that could stress them.

Soil Preparation and Protecting Plants from Pests

Preparing the soil is one of the most critical steps in cultivating robust cannabis plants. Healthy soil provides a solid foundation, ensuring that your plants receive the essential nutrients they need to thrive. However, it's not just about planting and watering; there are several crucial components to consider.

First, conducting soil tests is an indispensable part of the process. These tests help determine the pH levels and nutrient content of your soil, which is crucial for optimal growth. Cannabis prefers slightly acidic soil with a pH between 6.0 and 7.0. By testing your soil, you can identify any deficiencies or imbalances that need addressing before planting begins. This step ensures that your plants will start off on the right foot.

Once you have your soil test results, it's time to incorporate organic amendments. Adding compost is a great way to improve soil fertility and structure. Compost is rich in essential nutrients and beneficial microorganisms that support plant health. For instance, adding two to four inches of compost and mixing it into the top six to twelve inches of soil can create a nutrient-rich environment for your cannabis plants. Other amendments like worm castings, bone meal, and kelp meal also provide additional nutrients such as nitrogen, phosphorus, and potassium, which are vital for healthy plant growth.

Tilling and aeration are other critical components of soil preparation. Tilling helps break up compacted soil, allowing roots to penetrate more easily and access nutrients and water. Using tools like a garden fork or tiller can make this task more manageable. Aeration promotes better oxygen flow to the roots, which is essential for root respiration and overall plant health. It's best to till and aerate your soil a few weeks before planting to give it time to settle.

Identifying common pests and understanding how to protect your plants from them is equally important. Cannabis plants can be susceptible to various pests such as aphids, spider mites, and caterpillars. Regular monitoring allows you to spot issues early before they escalate. Companion planting is a natural method to deter pests. For example, planting marigolds around your cannabis can repel harmful insects due to their strong scent. Fencing can also protect plants from larger wildlife such as deer and rabbits. Introducing beneficial insects, like ladybugs, can help control pest populations naturally by preying on aphids and other detrimental bugs.

Organic pest management strategies are essential for maintaining a healthy garden without resorting to harmful chemicals. Insecticidal soaps and oils, such as neem oil, can effectively manage a wide range of pests. A simple recipe involves mixing one to two tablespoons of neem oil with a few drops of liquid soap in a gallon of water and spraying it on the plants. Additionally, DIY pest repellents like garlic or chili pepper sprays can be easy to prepare and use. For instance, blending garlic cloves with water, straining the mixture, and then diluting it with more water can make an effective spray that repels aphids and other pests due to its strong odor.

Consistent monitoring and adapting strategies are key to successful pest management. Keeping an eye on your plants daily can help you detect issues early and take immediate action. If you notice an increase in specific pests, you might need to adjust your approach, whether that means applying more insecticidal soap, introducing more beneficial insects, or trying a new DIY repellent.

Additionally, mulching can be a valuable practice for maintaining soil health and deterring pests. Organic mulches like straw, leaves, or grass clippings not only help retain soil moisture and regulate temperature but also create a physical barrier against many crawling insects. Over time, as mulch decomposes, it adds more organic matter to the soil, further enhancing its fertility.

For those who prefer a more hands-off approach, biocontrol agents can be highly effective. Predatory insects like lacewings and predatory mites can keep pest populations under control naturally. These tiny allies prey on common cannabis pests, reducing their numbers without the need for chemical interventions. Integrating these natural predators into your garden can create a balanced ecosystem where beneficial insects keep harmful ones in check.

Good hygiene practices in the garden can also prevent pest and disease outbreaks. Regularly cleaning and removing debris, dead leaves, and weeds eliminates potential habitats for pests. Proper spacing between plants ensures good air circulation, reducing the risk of mold and mildew, which are common problems in humid environments. Avoid overwatering, as excess moisture can attract fungus gnats and lead to root rot.

Furthermore, rotating crops each season can disrupt the life cycles of pests that might otherwise become established in your soil. This practice also prevents nutrient depletion, as different plants have varying nutrient needs and contributions to the soil.

Maintaining biodiversity within your garden not only makes it more visually appealing but also promotes a healthier growing environment. Planting a variety of species supports a balanced ecosystem that deters specific pests and attracts a broad range of beneficial insects. Healthy, diverse plantings are less likely to suffer significant damage from any one type of pest.

Concluding Thoughts

Growing cannabis outdoors can be a rewarding venture when you follow the right strategies. This chapter has guided you through the essential steps, from choosing an ideal location to understanding the importance of sunlight, accessibility, and surveillance. We've also discussed how to manage temperature and humidity levels, ensuring that your plants can thrive in various climates. Legal compliance is another critical factor to keep in mind, as it helps avoid any potential legal issues down the line. By considering these factors, you'll set yourself up for a fruitful gardening experience.

Soil preparation and pest protection are key components that contribute to healthy cannabis growth. Conducting soil tests, adding organic amendments, and ensuring proper aeration provide a solid foundation for your plants. Monitoring for pests and employing natural remedies like companion planting and beneficial insects can keep your garden thriving without harmful chemicals. By integrating these practices into your routine, you'll cultivate not just a successful cannabis garden but also a sustainable one. With these insights, you're now better equipped to embark on your own outdoor cannabis cultivation journey.

Reference List

Growing Cannabis Outdoors: Expert Tips and Tricks . (n.d.). SunMed Growers. https://www.sunmedgrowers.com/education-resources/blog/post/growing-cannabis-outdoors/

Mastering Organic Cannabis Cultivation: Essential Guide to Soil Preparation, Composting, Companion Planting, and Natural Pest Control Strategies - Ashleys Organic . (2024, June 1). https://ashleysorganic.com/organic-cannabis-cultivation/

Organic Pest & Disease Prevention for Marijuana Plants: Tips & Tricks | 2024 □□ . (2023, August 18). Seedsherenow.com. https://seedsherenow.com/organic-pest-and-disease-prevention-for-marijuana/

The Ultimate Guide to Growing Autoflowering Cannabis Outdoors | Fast Buds . (n.d.). 2fast4buds.com. Retrieved August 2, 2024, from https://2fast4buds.com/news/How-To-Grow-Autoflowering-Cannabis-Outdoors

Chapter Six

Nutrient Management

Managing nutrients is a key aspect of growing healthy and productive cannabis plants. Without the right balance of nutrients, it's difficult to achieve optimal growth, yield, and potency. That's why understanding how to properly manage what your plants need can make all the difference in your cultivation efforts.

In this chapter, we'll delve into both macronutrients and micronutrients that are essential for cannabis health. You will learn about specific nutrients like nitrogen, phosphorus, and potassium, along with secondary nutrients such as calcium and magnesium. We'll also cover the importance of minor micronutrients like iron and zinc. In addition, we'll talk about effective feeding regimens tailored to different growth stages and explore how to monitor pH levels for better nutrient absorption. By mastering these aspects, you'll be well-equipped to ensure your plants thrive from seedling to harvest.

Essential Macronutrients and Micronutrients

Understanding the critical nutrients needed for healthy cannabis growth lays a foundation for effective nutrient management. Ensuring that cannabis plants receive the proper nutrients is essential for maximizing yield and potency. Let's explore these vital nutrients, their roles, and how to manage them.

Cannabis plants require macronutrients like nitrogen (N), phosphorus (P), and potassium (K) in large amounts for optimal growth. Each of these plays a specific role in plant health.

Nitrogen is crucial for vegetative growth, as it helps build proteins, enzymes, and chlorophyll, which are key for photosynthesis. During the early stages of growth, higher levels of nitrogen promote lush, green foliage and robust stem development.

Phosphorus is essential for root growth and flower development. It aids in energy transfer within the plant through molecules like ATP. Adequate phosphorus ensures strong root systems and enhances the formation of flowers, which is critical during the bloom phase.

Potassium strengthens the plant's overall health by regulating water uptake and improving resistance to diseases. It plays a significant role in enzyme activation and the production of adenosine triphosphate (ATP), which powers various cellular functions. Potassium also helps with the movement of water, nutrients, and carbohydrates within the plant.

While macronutrients are vital, secondary nutrients like calcium, magnesium, and sulfur are also important. These nutrients support the functions of macronutrients, helping maintain a healthy structure and promoting growth.

Calcium strengthens cell walls, providing structural stability and preventing issues like blossom end rot. It acts as a messenger between cells, aiding in various physiological processes. Without sufficient calcium, plants can exhibit stunted growth and poor fruit production.

Magnesium is a core component of chlorophyll, necessary for photosynthesis. It also assists in enzyme activation and the transportation of other nutrients throughout the plant. Magnesium deficiency can cause yellowing leaves with green veins, hindering photosynthetic efficiency.

Sulfur is involved in the synthesis of essential oils and amino acids. It contributes to chlorophyll production and overall plant metabolism. A lack of sulfur can lead to stunted growth and yellowing of young leaves.

In addition to macronutrients and secondary nutrients, cannabis requires micronutrients in smaller quantities. Micronutrients like iron, manganese, zinc, copper, and boron are essential for metabolic processes and preventing deficiency symptoms.

Iron is crucial for chlorophyll production and functions as an electron carrier in photosynthesis. Iron deficiency often manifests as interveinal chlorosis, where the spaces between the leaf veins turn yellow while the veins remain green.

Manganese supports chlorophyll production and photosynthesis. It also aids in nitrogen assimilation and enzyme activation. Deficiencies can result in reduced growth and mottling of the leaves.

Zinc is vital for the synthesis of plant hormones that regulate growth and development. It plays a role in enzyme function and protein synthesis. Zinc deficiencies can cause stunted growth and distorted leaves.

Copper is involved in reproductive growth and strengthens stems and branches. It also aids in lignin formation, which reinforces cell walls. Copper deficiency may lead to the wilting of young shoots and dieback of leaves.

Boron is necessary for cell wall formation and membrane integrity. It assists in the transport of sugars and the development of new tissue. Boron deficiency can result in brittle stems, hollow stems, and poor pollen viability.

Balanced feeding is a cornerstone of nutrient management, ensuring that all essential nutrients are supplied in the right proportions. This balance prevents toxic buildup and nutrient lockout that can impede plant growth. Over-fertilizing with one nutrient can lead to deficiencies or toxicities in others, making balanced feeding crucial.

Implementing a nutrient regimen tailored to the plant's growth stages is essential. During the vegetative stage, a higher nitrogen ratio promotes leafy growth. As the plant transitions to flowering, reducing nitrogen while increasing phosphorus and potassium supports flower development.

Monitoring pH levels is also critical for nutrient absorption. Cannabis thrives in slightly acidic to neutral pH ranges. In soil, the ideal pH range is 6.0 to 6.5, while hydroponic setups should maintain a pH between 5.5 and 6.5. Deviations from these ranges can lock out essential nutrients, hindering plant health and productivity.

To effectively manage nutrients, growers must regularly test the growing medium and adjust feeding schedules based on the results. Visual symptoms of nutrient deficiencies, such as yellowing leaves or slow growth, should be addressed promptly. Soil testing kits and pH meters are valuable tools in maintaining optimal growing conditions.

Lastly, understanding the differences in nutrient needs based on genetics and growing environments can lead to better nutrient management. Indoor growers have more control over environmental factors and can customize nutrient solutions accordingly. Outdoor growers should consider soil composition and weather conditions when selecting nutrients.

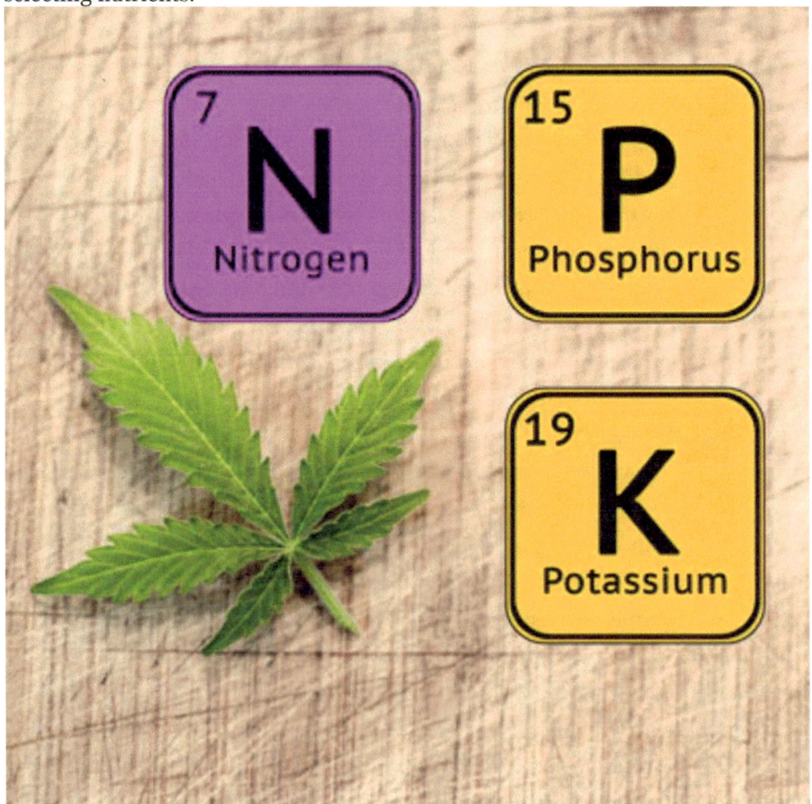

Organic vs. Synthetic Fertilizers and Feeding Schedules

Exploring the differences in fertilizer types helps cultivators make informed decisions based on their agricultural philosophy and goals. Organic fertilizers such as compost, manure, and fish emulsion promote soil health and provide a slow release of nutrients. These natural amendments are derived from plant, animal, or mineral-based compounds that undergo biochemical reactions, breaking down into soluble nutrients with the help of soil microbes. This process not only nourishes the plants but also enhances the soil's fertility by maintaining its structure and stimulating microbial activity. For instance, compost adds valuable organic matter to the soil, improving its texture and water retention capabilities. The gradual nutrient release ensures that plants receive a consistent supply of essential elements over time, reducing the risk of nutrient leaching and runoff.

On the other hand, synthetic fertilizers like NPK blends and liquid nutrients offer quick absorption but can lead to salt buildup and lack complex micronutrients. Synthetics are created through industrial processes and typically contain precise ratios of the primary nutrients: nitrogen, phosphorus, and potassium. Due to their water-soluble nature, these fertilizers provide an immediate boost to plant growth. However, this rapid nutrient availability can result in uneven growth spurts and may cause stress on plants if not applied correctly. For example, over-application of synthetic fertilizers can lead to root burn, where the high concentration of salts damages the delicate root structures. Moreover, synthetic fertilizers often lack the secondary and micronutrients necessary for a balanced plant diet, which means they might require supplementary additions to address specific deficiencies.

Implementing a feeding schedule tailored to growth stages is crucial for optimizing nutrient delivery throughout the plant's lifecycle. Cannabis plants, like many others, have distinct nutritional needs during various phases of growth—seedling, vegetative, and flowering stages. During the seedling stage, a light nutrient mix promotes root development. As the plant enters the vegetative phase, an increase in nitrogen supports lush, leafy growth. When the plant transitions to the flowering stage, higher levels of phosphorus and potassium aid in bud development and flower production. Creating a feeding schedule involves setting routine intervals for nutrient application and making environmental adjustments such as adjusting the pH levels of the growing medium and ensuring adequate water supply. By carefully monitoring and adjusting the nutrient regimen according to the plant's needs, growers can maximize yield and potency.

Recognizing symptoms of nutrient deficiencies through observation and soil testing is essential for maintaining plant health and preventing future issues. Plants exhibit specific signs when lacking certain nutrients; for instance, a nitrogen deficiency often manifests as yellowing leaves starting at the bottom of the plant, while phosphorus shortages can cause darkening and purpling of older leaves. Soil testing provides accurate information about the nutrient content and pH level of the growing medium, enabling growers to make precise adjustments. Prompt remedial actions such as adjusting the fertilizer composition or applying foliar sprays can quickly restore nutrient balance. Addressing deficiencies early prevents prolonged stress on the plants, which could hinder their development and reduce overall yields.

In choosing the right approach to fertilization, growers must consider their long-term goals and environmental impact. Organic fertilizers, with their ability to enhance soil health and sustainability, are often favored by those committed to eco-friendly cultivation practices. They create a resilient growing environment that benefits both the plants and the ecosystem. In contrast, synthetic fertilizers might appeal to growers looking for immediate results and simplicity in application. Despite their convenience, it's crucial to use them responsibly to avoid negative effects on soil health and surrounding water sources due to potential chemical runoff.

Ultimately, the choice between organic and synthetic fertilizers hinges on a grower's priorities and cultivation philosophy. If the goal is to foster a self-sustaining garden with a focus on long-term soil health, organic options may be more suitable. Conversely, if the objective is to achieve rapid growth and simplicity, synthetics might be preferred. Balancing the benefits and drawbacks of each type allows cultivators to craft a fertilization strategy that aligns with their specific needs and conditions.

To guide cultivators in making informed choices, it's beneficial to consider a few guidelines. First, assess the soil quality and existing nutrient levels before deciding on a fertilizer type. Understanding the baseline condition of the planting medium can inform whether organic amendments will suffice or if additional synthetic supplements are necessary. Second, start with smaller doses and gradually increase the application rates. This cautious approach helps avoid overwhelming the plants and allows for better monitoring of their responses. Third, integrate regular soil testing into the maintenance routine to track changes over time and adjust the nutrient plan accordingly. Lastly, stay observant and proactive in identifying any signs of nutrient imbalances, addressing them promptly to maintain optimal plant health.

Bringing It All Together

In this chapter, we've dived deep into the world of cannabis nutrients, uncovering the vital role that macronutrients and micronutrients play in healthy plant growth. We've learned how nitrogen fuels vegetative growth, phosphorus boosts root and flower development, and potassium fortifies overall plant health. Alongside these macronutrients, secondary nutrients like calcium, magnesium, and sulfur, plus an array of essential micronutrients, ensure that plants thrive by supporting various physiological functions. Balanced feeding is key to preventing toxic build-up and nutrient lockout, helping you manage your plants' needs effectively.

We also highlighted the importance of monitoring pH levels and regularly testing soil to adjust nutrient regimens based on specific results. Recognizing symptoms of nutrient deficiencies early ensures your plants stay healthy and productive. Whether you're growing indoors with precise control or navigating outdoor conditions, understanding your plants' nutritional needs at different growth stages allows for tailored nutrient management. By implementing these insights, you'll be well-equipped to maximize yield and potency, ensuring a rewarding cultivation experience.

Reference List

Cannabis Nutrients 101: Maximize Growth and Yield with Reiziger's Expert Tips . (2023, December 7). Reiziger. https://www.reiziger.com/cannabis-nutrients-101-maximizing-growth-and-yield/

CannaCon. (2020, March 27). *Essential Nutrients for Cannabis Growth* . CannaCon. https://cannacon.org/essential-nutrients-for-cannabis-growth/

Milorganite. (2019). *Organic vs Synthetic Fertilizer | Milorganite* . Milorganite.com. https://www.milorganite.com/lawn-care/organic-lawn-care/organic-vs-synthetic

Organic Vs. Synthetic Fertilizer: Pros, Cons, And Which To Use . (2024, May 3). Eos.com. https://eos.com/blog/organic-vs-synthetic-fertilizers/

Chapter Seven

Watering Practices

Watering practices play a crucial role in cannabis cultivation. Ensuring your plants receive the right amount of water at the right times can make all the difference between a thriving crop and one that's struggling. Without proper watering techniques, issues such as root rot, nutrient deficiencies, and moldy buds can arise, significantly impacting the overall health and yield of your plants.

In this chapter, we'll explore everything you need to know to master watering practices for your cannabis plants. We'll start by examining the specific watering needs during various growth stages: seedling, vegetative, and flowering. We'll then dive into the environmental factors like temperature, humidity, and light levels that influence water requirements. Additionally, we'll consider how plant size and pot size affect watering schedules, along with insights on different soil types and their impact on moisture retention. Finally, you'll learn practical methods to assess when it's time to water your plants, ensuring they remain healthy and vibrant throughout their growth cycle.

Determining Water Needs

Understanding the specific watering needs of cannabis plants throughout their growth stages is essential for any grower. Effective hydration practices not only enhance plant growth but also prevent common issues such as root rot and nutrient deficiencies.

Growth Stage Watering Needs

The water requirements of cannabis plants differ significantly across various growth stages—seedling, vegetative, and flowering. During the seedling stage, the young plants are delicate and require gentle misting to keep the soil consistently damp without overwatering. The seedlings' roots are fragile, and excess water can suffocate them.

As plants enter the vegetative stage, they experience rapid growth, necessitating an increase in water intake. Growers should aim to allow the top inch of soil to dry out between waterings to ensure that roots receive adequate oxygen. This period marks a critical phase where plants build their structural foundation through robust root development and leaf expansion.

Finally, during the flowering stage, cannabis plants reach their peak water demand. Similar to the vegetative stage, let the top 1-2 inches of soil dry out before the next watering session. Overwatering during this phase can lead to moldy buds or diseased roots, so it's often better to err on the side of under-watering.

Environmental Factors

Several environmental variables influence how much water cannabis plants need, namely temperature, humidity, and light levels. In warmer climates, higher temperatures accelerate water evaporation from both the soil and the plant, necessitating more frequent watering. Conversely, in cooler environments, water uptake slows down, and less frequent watering may be required.

Humidity levels also play a crucial role. High humidity can reduce the water requirement because the plants absorb moisture directly from the air, especially during the early stages. However, too much humidity can slow down overall plant development, requiring adjustments in watering practices. Low humidity, on the other hand, increases the rate of transpiration, prompting growers to water more often to compensate for the rapid moisture loss.

Light exposure has a dual effect on water needs. More intense light accelerates photosynthesis, leading to increased water consumption. Plants grown under high-intensity lights typically require more frequent watering compared to those exposed to natural or low-intensity light sources.

Plant Size and Pot Size Consideration

The size of the plant and its pot directly affects water requirements. Large cannabis plants with extensive foliage demand more water to sustain their physiological functions. Similarly, larger pots hold more soil, which can retain water longer, thereby reducing watering frequency. It's essential to tailor watering schedules based on these factors to avoid under or overwatering.

Smaller pots, although easier to manage, require more frequent watering since they retain less moisture and nutrients. They also leave less room for root growth, which could necessitate more careful monitoring and adjustments in watering routines.

Soil Type Impacts

Different soil types have varying capacities to retain moisture, affecting how much and how often you should water your cannabis plants. For instance, soil-based mediums generally offer good drainage, requiring growers to check the top inch of soil and water when it is dry. This method ensures thorough saturation without waterlogging the roots.

On the other hand, growing mediums like coco coir and peat moss retain moisture exceptionally well but need adequate aeration to prevent compaction and waterlogging. With coco coir, maintaining proper air flow while ensuring consistent moisture levels is key. Peat moss can become compacted over time, so it's crucial to monitor and maintain its texture to facilitate proper drainage.

In hydroponic systems, the precision of water supply and nutrient infusion becomes critical. These systems usually employ inert growing media like clay pellets or rock wool, which provide excellent aeration but have different water retention properties. Clay pellets dry out quickly, necessitating consistent moisture checks, while rock wool retains less water and requires regular watering to maintain optimal conditions.

Other materials like vermiculite and perlite also impact watering requirements. Vermiculite retains moisture efficiently but can easily become waterlogged if overwatered. Perlite offers excellent drainage but holds little moisture, so it demands regular monitoring to ensure plants don't dry out.

By understanding these distinct characteristics and adjusting your watering practices accordingly, you can create an environment that supports healthy, thriving cannabis plants at every growth stage.

Assessing When to Water

Determining the right time to water your cannabis plants is just as important as knowing how much water they need. Simple methods like the finger test, where you insert your index finger into the soil up to the first knuckle, can offer a quick assessment of soil moisture. If the soil feels dry, it's time to water; if damp, wait a day or two before testing again.

Another effective technique is the weighing pots method. By lifting the plant's container regularly, you'll develop an intuitive sense of whether the pot feels lighter, indicating the need for water, or heavier, suggesting sufficient moisture levels.

For those seeking more precise measurements, moisture meters can provide accurate readings of soil moisture content. Insert the probe into the soil, and the meter will indicate whether the soil is dry, moist, or wet, enabling more informed watering decisions.

Conclusion

Types of Water and Irrigation Systems

When it comes to watering cannabis plants, the type of water you choose can significantly impact their growth and overall health. Tap water is a common choice for many home growers due to its convenience and availability. However, it's important to understand both the benefits and drawbacks of using municipal water sources. One major advantage of tap water is that it's easily accessible and doesn't require additional costs or effort to obtain. Many municipalities also add chlorine or chloramine to tap water, which can help prevent harmful bacteria and pathogens from affecting your plants.

On the downside, tap water often contains various minerals and chemicals that may not be ideal for cannabis cultivation. High levels of calcium, magnesium, and other minerals can lead to nutrient imbalances in the soil, potentially causing deficiencies or toxicities in your plants. To mitigate these issues, you can leave tap water out for 24 hours to allow chlorine to evaporate or use a water filter to remove unwanted minerals and chemicals.

Distilled water offers another alternative for cannabis cultivation. This type of water undergoes a purification process that removes all minerals, chemicals, and contaminants, making it an excellent choice for growers who want to have complete control over their plants' nutrient intake. The absence of any impurities ensures that you can add exactly the right amount of nutrients without worrying about imbalances caused by unknown elements in the water.

However, distilled water can be more expensive and less environmentally friendly than other options. It requires energy to produce and often comes in plastic containers, contributing to waste. Additionally, because distilled water is devoid of minerals, you'll need to be diligent in providing a balanced nutrient solution to compensate for the lack of natural minerals that might otherwise support plant health.

Drip irrigation systems are highly effective for delivering consistent moisture directly to the root zone of your cannabis plants. These systems use emitters to release small amounts of water slowly and precisely, ensuring that each plant receives the right amount of water without oversaturating the soil. One of the main advantages of drip irrigation is its water efficiency. By targeting the root area directly, you minimize water wastage due to evaporation and runoff. This method is particularly beneficial in conserving water in areas with limited water resources or stringent water usage regulations.

In addition to water conservation, drip irrigation systems also promote optimal nutrient uptake. Since the water is delivered directly to the roots, it can be combined with fertigation – the process of adding nutrients into the irrigation water. This allows for precise control over nutrient delivery, leading to healthier and more productive plants. However, it's essential to maintain the system regularly to prevent clogging of emitters and lines, especially if your water source has high sediment content.

Automatic timers complement drip irrigation systems brilliantly by further streamlining the watering process. These timers can be programmed to turn the irrigation system on and off at specific times, ensuring that your plants are consistently watered according to their needs. Automatic timers are especially useful for busy growers or those managing larger cultivation operations, as they eliminate the guesswork and labor involved in manual watering.

By automating the irrigation schedule, you can avoid common watering pitfalls such as under-watering or over-watering, both of which can stress the plants and hinder their growth. Moreover, automatic timers provide flexibility in adjusting watering frequency based on seasonal changes or different stages of plant development. For instance, during the flowering stage when plants require more frequent watering, you can easily modify the timer settings to accommodate this increased demand.

While setting up a drip irrigation system with automatic timers requires an initial investment, the long-term benefits in terms of water efficiency, labor savings, and improved plant health make it a worthwhile consideration for serious cannabis cultivators. Regular maintenance, such as checking for leaks and cleaning emitters, will ensure the system functions optimally and delivers the desired results.

Water temperature is also a critical factor that should not be overlooked in cannabis cultivation. The temperature of the water you use can affect nutrient uptake and overall plant health. Ideally, water should be at room temperature, around 68°F to 72°F (20°C to 22°C). Using water that is too cold can shock the roots, slowing down metabolic processes and potentially causing root diseases. Conversely, excessively hot water can cause root damage and reduce oxygen levels in the water, which are vital for healthy root respiration.

Monitoring water temperature is essential, especially if you draw water from outdoor sources where temperature fluctuations can occur. In colder climates, consider using a water heater or storing water containers indoors to stabilize the temperature before watering your plants. Similarly, in hot conditions, allowing the water to cool down to room temperature before application can prevent heat stress on the roots. By maintaining an appropriate water temperature, you create a more conducive environment for nutrient absorption and robust plant growth.

Wrapping Up

Understanding the watering needs of your cannabis plants is crucial for their healthy growth and successful cultivation. In this chapter, we've explored how different stages of growth—seedling, vegetative, and flowering—require specific watering practices to prevent overwatering or underwatering. Environmental factors like temperature, humidity, and light levels also play significant roles in determining how often you should water your plants. By tailoring your watering schedule accordingly, you can ensure your plants get the right amount of hydration to thrive.

We also discussed how plant size, pot size, and soil type impact water retention and uptake. Using tools like the finger test, weighing pots, and moisture meters can help you decide when it's time to water. Choosing the right type of water, whether it's tap, distilled, or filtered, along with considering irrigation systems like drip irrigation with automatic timers, provides efficient ways to keep your plants well-watered. These insights aim to empower hobbyist gardeners, medical cannabis patients, and anyone interested in cannabis cultivation to grow healthier, more productive plants.

Reference List

Cannabis Watering Guide [2024]: How to Prevent Problems . (n.d.). SunMed Growers. https://www.sunmedgrowers.com/education-resources/blog/post/cannabis-watering-guide/

Different Irrigation Systems for Cannabis: Pros and Cons . (n.d.). Floraflex.com. Retrieved August 2, 2024, from https://floraflex.com/UK/blog/post/different-irrigation-systems-for-cannabis-pros-and-cons

Pros And Cons Of Cannabis Irrigation Systems . (n.d.). Growcycle.com. Retrieved August 2, 2024, from https://growcycle.com/learn/pros-and-cons-of-cannabis-irrigation-systems

admin. (2022, November 5). *Watering Cannabis Plants: Your Ultimate Guide* . Smart Watering an Autonomous Drip Irrigation System. https://smart-watering.com/2022/11/05/watering-cannabis-plants-how-to/

Chapter Eight

Pest and Disease Control

Managing pests and diseases in cannabis cultivation is a vital part of ensuring healthy plants without relying on harmful chemicals. Understanding how to keep these nuisances at bay with natural methods not only protects the plant but also supports a more sustainable and eco-friendly growing practice. In this chapter, readers will dive into the world of pest and disease management, discovering how different strategies can be used to protect their crops naturally while maintaining robust plant health.

The chapter delves deep into identifying common cannabis pests like aphids, spider mites, and whiteflies and offers practical tips for control and prevention. By spotlighting beneficial insects, such as ladybugs and parasitoid wasps, and explaining the use of organic solutions like neem oil, readers gain an arsenal of tools for managing pest problems. Additionally, the chapter covers essential practices to prevent diseases like powdery mildew and root rot, promoting techniques that help create a healthier growing environment. From integrated pest management (IPM) strategies to fostering a balanced ecosystem, readers will learn comprehensive approaches to safeguard their cannabis plants through natural and effective means.

Common Cannabis Pests and Natural Pest Control Solutions

In our quest to nurture healthy cannabis plants, understanding and managing common pests is crucial. Let's delve into identifying these pests and employing environmentally friendly methods to keep them at bay.

Aphids: These small insects are notorious for sucking the sap from plant tissues, which significantly reduces the vigor of cannabis plants. Aphid infestations typically manifest as curling leaves and a noticeable decrease in plant health. One effective way to manage aphids is by attracting their natural predators, such as ladybugs. Ladybugs are voracious eaters of aphids, with a single ladybug capable of consuming up to 50 aphids daily. Introducing these beneficial insects into your garden can help maintain a balanced ecosystem and naturally reduce aphid populations. Additionally, aphid damage can be minimized by regularly inspecting your plants and removing infested leaves to prevent the spread.

Spider Mites: Tiny yet highly destructive, spider mites cause leaf discoloration and characteristic webbing on cannabis plants. These arachnids thrive in dry, dusty conditions, so maintaining optimal humidity levels is vital in preventing infestations. If spider mites do appear, neem oil is an excellent organic remedy. Neem oil contains azadirachtin, which inhibits the growth and reproduction of these pests. To apply neem oil effectively, mix it at the recommended dilution ratio (usually about 1-2 tablespoons per gallon of water) and spray it on the affected plants during the evening to avoid direct sunlight. Consistent application every few days will help suppress the mite population and allow your plants to recover.

Whiteflies: These small, winged insects can cause significant damage to cannabis plants by leaving behind a sticky residue known as honeydew, which attracts sooty mold. Early detection is key to controlling whiteflies. Regularly inspect the undersides of leaves where they commonly lay eggs. Yellow sticky traps are useful tools for monitoring and reducing whitefly populations. Place these traps around your garden to capture adult whiteflies, thus interrupting their life cycle. Additionally, introducing parasitoid wasps, which lay their eggs inside whitefly nymphs, can provide biological control and further reduce whitefly numbers.

Neem Oil: An organic pesticide revered for its effectiveness against various cannabis pests, neem oil is a staple in sustainable gardening. It's not just useful against spider mites but also works well against aphids, whiteflies, and other pests. Neem oil's versatility stems from its ability to disrupt insect feeding and reproduction while being relatively safe for beneficial insects like ladybugs and bees. When using neem oil, it's essential to follow proper application guidelines. During the vegetative stage, a dilution ratio of 1-2 tablespoons per gallon of water is ideal. Apply this solution as a foliar spray every 7-14 days. For plants in the flowering stage, exercise caution; applying neem oil too close to harvest can affect the taste of your buds. Cease neem applications at least three weeks before harvesting to ensure no residue remains. (Talerico, 2019; *Learn How to Use Neem Oil to Fight Cannabis Pests - RQS Blog*, n.d.)

Fungus Gnats: Though not explicitly part of our primary list, fungus gnats deserve mention due to their potential damage. The larvae live in soil and can harm root systems, leading to stunted plant growth and reduced yields. Implementing good watering practices helps prevent fungus gnat infestations. Overwatering promotes the moist conditions that fungus gnats favor, so allow the top layer of soil to dry out between watering sessions. Introducing beneficial nematodes, microscopic worms that prey on gnat larvae, can also be a practical approach to managing these pests organically.

In addition to specific pest control methods, fostering a healthy growing environment is the best defense against pests. This begins with maintaining biodynamic, living organic soil rich in nutrients and beneficial microorganisms. Regularly amending your soil with compost or organic fertilizers will support plant health and resilience. Ensuring adequate airflow around your plants by spacing them appropriately and pruning lower foliage helps create an unfavorable environment for many pests.

Disease Prevention and Integrated Pest Management (IPM) Strategies

When cultivating cannabis, one of the most critical aspects of ensuring a healthy and bountiful harvest is mastering pest and disease control without resorting to harmful chemicals. This involves understanding common pitfalls like powdery mildew and root rot, as well as adopting comprehensive integrated pest management (IPM) strategies. These approaches will help in preventing diseases, ensuring a robust growth environment, and maintaining plant health.

One major challenge that cannabis cultivators face is powdery mildew. This fungal disease is characterized by white, powdery spots on the leaves, which can quickly spread if not addressed. It thrives in high humidity, making environmental control crucial for prevention. Cultivators should aim to keep humidity levels below 50%, especially during the flowering stage when plants are most vulnerable. Adequate ventilation and proper spacing between plants also enhance airflow, reducing the likelihood of an outbreak. Regularly inspecting the leaves and stems for early signs allows for prompt action, such as pruning affected areas and applying organic fungicides like neem oil or potassium bicarbonate.

Root rot presents another significant issue, often caused by overwatering and poor drainage. Symptoms include wilting, yellowing leaves, and a mushy root system with a foul odor. Preventing root rot starts with using well-draining soil or growing mediums. Containers should have sufficient drainage holes, and watering practices must be adjusted to avoid waterlogged conditions. Incorporating beneficial bacteria and mycorrhizae into the soil can help protect against root pathogens by promoting a healthy root zone. For growers dealing with early signs of root rot, treatments such as hydrogen peroxide solutions can be employed to oxygenate the roots and kill off pathogenic microbes.

Effective pest control requires diligent monitoring and scouting. Regular inspections of plants can detect early signs of pests before they become a major problem. This routine should include checking the undersides of leaves, stems, and soil surface for insects or their eggs. Using a magnifying glass can aid in spotting tiny pests like spider mites. Keeping a detailed pest journal helps track findings and monitor trends, allowing growers to respond promptly and appropriately. Sticky traps can also be used around the grow area to capture flying insects and serve as an additional monitoring tool.

Another key element in successful pest management is understanding thresholds for action. Not all pests require immediate intervention; some can be tolerated at low levels without significant harm to the plants. Therefore, it is essential to set acceptable limits for various pests based on their potential impact. For instance, while a few aphids might not cause noticeable damage, an infestation would warrant action. Thresholds can vary depending on the growth stage of the plant and the specific pest involved. Establishing these thresholds helps in making informed decisions about whether to apply control measures or wait and continue monitoring.

To further bolster disease prevention, starting with healthy plants is paramount. Cultivators should source high-quality seeds or clones from reputable suppliers, ensuring they are free from diseases. Testing mother plants and seedlings for common pathogens before introducing them into the grow space can prevent the spread of infections. Screening new plants using advanced methods like qPCR detection assays can identify asymptomatic carriers of diseases, enabling early intervention.

Optimizing growing conditions is another preventive measure. Environmental factors such as temperature, humidity, and airflow should be kept within optimal ranges for cannabis growth. Consistent temperatures between 68-77°F (20-25°C) and maintaining relative humidity levels appropriate for the plant's growth stage—higher during vegetative and lower during flowering—are crucial. Proper ventilation reduces moisture buildup and prevents conditions conducive to fungal diseases.

Sanitation practices cannot be overlooked in preventing the spread of pathogens. Regularly cleaning and sanitizing equipment, tools, and surfaces in the grow space minimizes cross-contamination risks. Using separate tools for each plant or disinfecting tools between uses further reduces the chance of spreading infections from one plant to another. It's also advisable to sterilize hands or wear gloves when handling plants, particularly after contact with any potentially infected material.

Implementing a comprehensive IPM plan integrates cultural, mechanical, biological, and chemical control methods to manage pests and diseases effectively while minimizing environmental impact. Cultural controls involve altering growing practices and conditions to reduce pest problems, such as crop rotation and selecting disease-resistant cultivars. Mechanical controls include physical barriers like insect screens and manual removal of pests. Biological controls use natural predators or beneficial organisms to keep pest populations in check. Organic pesticides, though used sparingly, provide a last-resort solution when other methods aren't sufficient.

For cultivators aiming to refine their practices continually, ongoing education is vital. Staying updated on common cannabis diseases, their symptoms, and effective management strategies through reputable sources is essential. Engaging with the cannabis growing community via forums and attending relevant events can offer fresh insights and practical advice.

Final Insights

This chapter has armed you with practical strategies to manage pests and diseases in your cannabis garden without turning to harmful chemicals. We've explored how to handle common pests like aphids, spider mites, and whiteflies using natural methods such as introducing beneficial insects, maintaining proper humidity levels, and using neem oil. Additionally, we've emphasized the importance of fostering a healthy growing environment, from ensuring good soil health to optimizing airflow around your plants.

You now have a toolkit full of integrated pest management strategies to keep your cannabis plants thriving. By understanding the signs of potential problems and taking proactive steps, you can prevent issues before they get out of hand. Remember, maintaining vigilance through regular inspections and being mindful of your growing conditions will create a resilient garden. With these insights, you're well on your way to cultivating robust, healthy cannabis plants organically.

Reference List

Amirault, B. (2024, May 7). *Cannabis Crop Diseases | Prevention Strategies* . Medicinal Genomics. https://medicinalgenomics.com/cannabis-crop-diseases-proven-prevention-strategies/

Liam Buirs, & Punja, Z. K. (2024, March 10). *Integrated Management of Pathogens and Microbes in Cannabis sativa L. (Cannabis) under Greenhouse Conditions* . Plants; Multidisciplinary Digital Publishing Institute. https://doi.org/10.3390/plants13060786

Learn How to Use Neem Oil to Fight Cannabis Pests - RQS Blog . (n.d.). Royal Queen Seeds. Retrieved August 2, 2024, from https://www.royalqueenseeds.com/us/blog-neem-oil-the-organic-pesticide-of-choice-for-cannabis-n657

Talerico, D. (2019, June 28). *Organic Cannabis Pest Control: How to Keep Bugs Off Your Nugs* . Homestead and Chill. https://homesteadandchill.com/organic-cannabis-pest-control-bugs-off-nugs/

Chapter Nine

Training and Pruning Techniques

Training and pruning techniques are essential for any grower looking to optimize plant structure and yields. These methods help shape the plants into more productive and healthier versions of themselves, ensuring that you get the most out of your cultivation efforts. By understanding and applying these techniques, you can transform your garden into a thriving oasis of greenery.

In this chapter, we will explore various methods of training and pruning, such as topping and FIMming, which encourage bushier growth and increased bud sites. We will delve into low-stress training (LST) for manipulating plant growth without causing significant stress and discuss the Screen of Green (ScrOG) technique to maximize light exposure and airflow. Each method will be explained in detail, providing step-by-step guidance on how to implement them effectively in your growing setup. Whether you're a hobbyist gardener or someone interested in the benefits of cannabis cultivation, these insights will help you take your gardening skills to the next level.

Topping and FIMming

Topping and FIMming are two essential techniques in the art of plant training that can significantly enhance growth and yield by encouraging bushier plants. Understanding these methods allows growers to optimize their cultivation practices, ensuring healthier plants with more abundant harvests.

Let's dive into topping first. This technique involves cutting off the top of the main stem of the plant. By doing this, you disrupt the natural apical dominance, which is the tendency of the plant to grow a single, dominant main stem. When the top is removed, the plant redirects its energy to the lateral branches. These side branches now have the potential to grow more vigorously, creating multiple new bud sites. The result is a bushier plant with an increased number of colas, or clusters of buds, which can potentially lead to higher yields. Another benefit of topping is the promotion of denser foliage, as the internodal spacing - the distance between the nodes on the stem - becomes shorter. This denser growth supports more flowers and makes for a sturdier plant structure capable of handling heavier bud production.

In contrast, the FIMming technique, which stands for "Fuck, I Missed," is a more subtle variation of topping. Instead of completely removing the top part of the main stem, only a portion of it is pinched off. This partial removal results in less stress for the plant while still promoting lateral branch development. With FIMming, the plant can develop multiple main stems rather than just one or two, leading to a broader, more robust canopy. This method often yields higher overall plant mass and is gentler on the plant, allowing for quicker recovery compared to topping.

Timing is critical for both topping and FIMming to ensure minimal stress and maximized growth response. Best practices suggest performing these techniques during the late vegetative stage. At this point, the plant is mature enough to handle the pruning but not yet at the flowering stage, where such disruptions could negatively impact bud development. Executing these techniques too early may stunt the plant's growth, while doing it too late might not provide enough time for the plant to recover and redirect its energy efficiently.

Once you've topped or FIMmed your plants, it's essential to follow up with proper pruning to maximize the benefits of these techniques. Regular pruning days should be scheduled to remove excessive foliage that can overshadow bud sites. By trimming away unproductive leaves and branches, the plant can focus its energy on producing buds instead of maintaining unnecessary foliage. Additionally, maintaining a healthy leaf-to-light ratio ensures that all parts of the plant receive adequate light exposure, promoting even growth and reducing the risk of mold or pest infestations.

After utilizing these techniques, some specific guidelines can help maintain optimal plant health. For topping, make sure to use clean, sharp pruning shears to make a precise cut just above a node, ensuring there are two or more healthy nodes below the cut. This promotes more robust branching from those nodes. For FIMming, using your fingers to pinch off approximately 75% of the new growth tip can often be more effective. The goal here is to leave a small portion of the growth intact, encouraging multiple new shoots to emerge from the pinched point.

Combining topping or FIMming with other training techniques like low-stress training (LST) or scrogging can further enhance yield potential and shape the plant's structure. LST involves gently bending and securing branches to create a more even canopy, allowing for better light penetration and airflow. Scrogging uses a screen to spread out the plant's branches, again maximizing light exposure and promoting uniform growth across the canopy.

It's also crucial to monitor the environmental conditions after performing these techniques. Optimal temperatures, humidity levels, and adequate lighting are key factors in ensuring the plant's recovery and continued growth. Stress from suboptimal conditions can negate the benefits of topping and FIMming, emphasizing the importance of a controlled growing environment.

Understanding the balance between topping and FIMming is important for growers. While both techniques aim to promote bushier growth and increase bud sites, choosing between them depends on individual growing conditions and goals. Topping provides a more pronounced effect on lateral branching but comes with greater stress to the plant. On the other hand, FIMming offers a gentler approach that allows for multiple main stems and potentially quicker recovery, although it might require more precision and patience to execute correctly.

In practical terms, consider performing a combination of both techniques on different plants within the same crop cycle to observe their effects directly. This hands-on experimentation can offer valuable insights into which method works best under your specific growing conditions. Furthermore, keeping detailed records of each plant's response to these techniques can aid in refining your approach over time, leading to more consistent and predictable results.

In summary, topping and FIMming are powerful tools in a grower's toolkit. By carefully removing the top parts of the plant, whether fully or partially, you can encourage lateral growth, increase the number of bud sites, and ultimately improve the yield and quality of your crops. Timing these techniques during the late vegetative stage and following up with regular pruning and optimal environmental conditions will ensure your plants thrive. Experimenting with both methods and integrating them with other training techniques can further fine-tune your cultivation practices, helping you achieve the best possible outcomes.

Low Stress Training (LST)

Low Stress Training (LST) is an effective method for manipulating the growth of plants without causing significant stress. This technique is particularly useful for cannabis cultivation, where optimizing plant structure and maximizing yields are crucial. Let's dive into the core concepts and applications of LST to understand its benefits and how it can be implemented effectively.

The basic principles of LST revolve around encouraging multiple bud sites to form an even canopy structure. Unlike high-stress techniques such as topping or pruning, LST involves gently bending and securing the stems of the plant using flexible ties or weights. This approach helps in distributing light more evenly across the plant, reducing the need for aggressive pruning. By guiding the stems to grow in desired directions, growers can manipulate the plant's shape and ensure that all parts receive adequate light and airflow. The result is a healthier plant with multiple colas, leading to increased bud production.

To implement LST, it's important to start early, ideally when the plant is still young and flexible. Early training allows for better manipulation of the plant's structure, leading to more uniform growth. Starting early also reduces the risk of breaking stems, which can occur if the plant becomes too rigid. Visual illustrations can be extremely helpful for beginners to grasp different training methods. These visuals can show how to bend and secure the stems properly without causing damage. For instance, using garden wires, soft ties, or twine can help in maintaining the desired shape of the plant.

One of the main benefits of LST over traditional methods is that it minimizes shock to the plant. Techniques like topping involve cutting off the top growth, which can temporarily stunt the plant's development. In contrast, LST allows for continuous growth by merely redirecting the stems. This gentle approach ensures that the plant remains healthy and productive. Additionally, LST can be easily integrated with other training methods. For example, combining LST with techniques like ScrOG (Screen of Green) can further enhance light distribution and maximize yields.

Maintaining the LST structure requires regular adjustments to balance oxygen and light distribution. As the plant grows, the stems will naturally try to revert to their original positions. Regularly checking and readjusting the ties or weights can help maintain the optimal angles for each branch. Growers should also monitor the plant for signs of stress, such as drooping leaves or discolored stems. These signs may indicate that the ties are too tight or that the plant needs more time to recover between adjustments.

Balancing oxygen and light distribution is critical for the plant's overall health. Ensuring that all parts of the plant receive adequate light helps in promoting even growth and preventing any single part from becoming too dominant. Proper airflow around the plant reduces the risk of mold and pest infestations, which can be detrimental to the crop. Regular adjustment of the LST setup ensures that the plant continues to thrive and produce high-quality buds.

Another advantage of LST is its ability to keep plants discreet. By training the plant to grow horizontally rather than vertically, growers can maintain a lower profile. This is particularly useful for outdoor guerrilla grows where stealth is essential. Keeping the plant at the same height as surrounding vegetation makes it harder to detect. Indoors, LST helps manage space constraints by preventing plants from outgrowing their designated areas. This control over plant height and shape is invaluable for maximizing the efficiency of indoor growing setups.

LST also promotes even ripening of buds. Since all parts of the plant receive equal light exposure, the buds tend to mature simultaneously. This synchronization simplifies the harvesting process, as growers can collect the entire yield in one go rather than staggering the harvest over several days. Uniform ripening also means that all buds have a similar potency and quality, enhancing the overall value of the crop.

In implementing LST, it's vital to use appropriate materials. Garden wires, soft plant ties, and twine are excellent choices for securing the stems without causing damage. Avoid using materials that can cut into the plant, such as fishing lines or thin strings. The ties should be loose enough to accommodate the plant's growth but secure enough to hold the stems in place. Regularly checking the ties and adjusting them as needed can prevent constriction and ensure the plant's continued health.

Additionally, LST is suitable for both indoor and outdoor cultivation. Whether growing in a controlled indoor environment or an open outdoor space, this technique can be adapted to fit the specific needs of the plants. For indoor growers, LST helps optimize limited space by controlling the plant's height and shape. Outdoor growers benefit from the ability to keep plants within a discrete height range, blending in with surrounding vegetation.

Screen of Green (ScrOG)

To provide insights on using the Screen of Green (ScrOG) technique in a controlled growing environment, we'll explore its principles, setup process, growth management strategies, and overall benefits.

The ScrOG method involves using a mesh screen to spread out plant branches, which enhances light penetration, improves airflow, and helps manage plant height in small spaces. This technique allows growers to optimize their yields by ensuring that every part of the plant receives sufficient light and nutrients. The primary goal here is to create an even canopy where each bud site can thrive without being overshadowed.

Setting up a ScrOG system begins with selecting the right materials. A good quality screen or net with appropriate hole sizes is crucial. The holes should be large enough to allow branches to pass through but tight enough to support their weight. Trellis nets or pre-made ScrOG kits are commonly used, but you can also make your own from basic materials like string and stakes. Next, timing the installation is essential. Plants should be ready for training when they reach a certain height, typically during the vegetative stage. At this point, they are still flexible enough to be manipulated without causing damage.

Visual aids are particularly helpful during setup. They guide you in properly placing the screen and weaving the branches through it. First, position the screen about 8-12 inches above the base of the plants. As the plants grow, gently bend and tuck the branches under the screen. The goal is to encourage lateral growth and spread the branches horizontally across the net. This way, you create more bud sites and promote an even distribution of light.

Once your ScrOG system is set up, managing growth becomes an ongoing task. Regular checks are necessary to ensure that branches remain in their designated places and continue to receive adequate light. Adjust branches as needed to fill any gaps in the canopy and prevent any single area from becoming too dense. It's important to maintain an even canopy height; this ensures that all bud sites get equal exposure to light, which is critical for uniform growth and maximum yield.

Additionally, keeping growth within height constraints is vital. ScrOG is especially beneficial in confined growing setups where vertical space is limited. By training the plants to grow horizontally, you can maximize the available space and control the plant's height, which is particularly useful for indoor cultivation or grow tents.

However, while ScrOG offers numerous advantages, it also comes with considerations that require careful management. One significant benefit of ScrOG is that it increases the number of bud sites exposed to light and nutrients. This results in higher yields compared to traditional growing methods. Moreover, improved airflow reduces the risk of mold and mildew, promoting healthier plant development.

Despite these benefits, the ScrOG technique demands constant attention. Overgrowth can become an issue if not monitored closely, leading to tangled branches that are difficult to manage. This can obstruct light penetration and airflow, negating the very advantages ScrOG is supposed to provide. Regular pruning and trimming may be necessary to keep the plant growth in check and maintain the optimal structure of the canopy.

Summary and Reflections

By mastering topping and FIMming, you've learned how to shape your plants for better growth and bigger yields. These techniques not only help in creating bushier plants but also increase the number of bud sites, leading to a more abundant harvest. Remember, timing is everything. Performing these methods in the late vegetative stage ensures your plants can handle the stress and bounce back stronger. Following up with regular pruning keeps them healthy and maximizes light exposure.

Combining these training methods with other techniques like LST or ScrOG can further optimize your growing setup. Trying out different approaches lets you see what works best for your specific conditions. Keep detailed notes on each plant's response to the various techniques to refine your process over time. With patience and practice, you'll be able to create a thriving garden that meets your needs, whether you're a hobbyist gardener, medical cannabis patient, or someone interested in the plant's wellness benefits.

Reference List

Collado, E. (2022, May 3). *Performing Low Stress Training Technique to cannabis plants* . Blog de Grow Barato. https://www.growbarato.net/blog/en/low-stress-training-lst-marijuana-growing-techniques/

Cannabis Pruning Guide: Fimming vs Topping for Optimal Results . (n.d.). Altaqua.com. Retrieved August 2, 2024, from https://altaqua.com/fimming-vs-topping/

Cannabis Low Stress Training (LST) Tutorial . (n.d.). Grow Weed Easy. Retrieved August 2, 2024, from https://www.growweedeasy.com/low-stress-training-lst

Exploring the Benefits of Topping and FIMing for Higher Cannabis Yields . (n.d.). Floraflex.com. Retrieved August 2, 2024, from https://floraflex.com/EU/blog/post/exploring-the-benefits-of-topping-and-fiming-for-higher-cannabis-yields

Everything About SCROG Method: When and How to Do It . (n.d.). Hey Abby. Retrieved August 2, 2024, from https://heyabby.com/blogs/articles/guide-to-scrog-method

Vee. (2024, May 15). *Mastering the SCROG (Screen of Green) Methods: A Comprehensive Guide* . https://vivosun.com/growing_guide/scrog-guide/

Chapter Ten

Flowering Stage and Harvest Timing

Understanding the flowering stage and optimal harvest timing is central to producing high-quality cannabis. During this exciting phase, plants reveal their potential as they begin to flower, signaling a critical period for growers to pay close attention. Whether you're nurturing your first plant or refining your skills, grasping the nuances of this stage can transform your gardening experience. As the plant transitions from its vegetative phase, it undergoes remarkable changes in appearance and growth patterns, setting the stage for the development of potent buds.

In this chapter, we will explore the key indicators that mark the beginning of the flowering stage, including the emergence of pistils and changes in the plant's structure. You'll learn how to adjust care routines and manipulate light cycles to support healthy flowering, whether you're growing indoors or outdoors. Moreover, we'll delve into the science of trichome development, providing insights into how these tiny structures dictate the right time to harvest. By understanding and monitoring trichomes, you'll be able to optimize the potency and quality of your final product, ensuring that your efforts yield the best possible results.

Recognizing the Start of Flowering

Cannabis plants go through several stages of growth, with the flowering phase being one of the most crucial stages for ensuring a bountiful and potent harvest. Recognizing the signs that indicate the onset of this phase can significantly help growers to customize their care routine, thereby maximizing yield and quality.

The pre-flowering stage is the initial indication that your cannabis plant is about to enter its flowering phase. This stage is characterized by key changes in the plant's appearance and growth patterns. One of the first indicators is the emergence of pistils—tiny white hairs that appear at the nodes where branches meet the stem. These pistils will later develop into buds. Additionally, you'll notice that the plant might start to stretch; it begins growing taller rapidly as it prepares to support large flowers. Another sign includes the development of pre-flowers, small formations that look like miniature versions of the buds yet to come. Observing these changes allows growers to adjust their care routines accordingly, such as altering nutrient mixes or light schedules.

Another critical aspect influencing the initiation of the flowering stage is the light cycle. For cannabis plants, particularly those grown outdoors, changes in daylight hours play a pivotal role. Photoperiodic cannabis strains depend on shifts from longer days to shorter days to trigger flowering. As the days get shorter, typically after the summer solstice, the plants naturally sense this change and begin their flowering process. For indoor cultivation, growers need to manually alter the light cycle to mimic this natural transition. Switching the light schedule from an 18-hour day and 6-hour night (18/6) to a 12-hour day and 12-hour night (12/12) will signal the plants to start flowering. This scheduling trick is essential for photoperiodic strains, which otherwise would continue vegetative growth indefinitely under prolonged light conditions.

Subtle morphological changes in cannabis plants also serve as indicators of readiness for the flowering stage. As mentioned, the rapid vertical growth known as "stretching" is a significant cue. Besides stretching, you may observe that the spaces between nodes—where branches intersect the main stem—start to grow closer together. The leaves at the top of the plant may also become narrower and more pointed. If you're growing regular seeds, it's around this time you can determine the sex of your plants, as males will produce pollen sacs while females develop pistils. Identifying these changes early can enable timely interventions, such as removing male plants to prevent pollination if producing sinsemilla (seedless female flowers) is the goal.

Cannabis plants have specific photoperiod requirements that vary depending on whether they are grown indoors or outdoors. Understanding these requirements is vital, especially for outdoor cultivators. Cannabis, being a short-day plant, needs long nights to flower. Outdoor growers must be aware of their local climate and daylight patterns to plan the planting and harvesting times effectively. For example, in regions like California, farmers need to consider the seasonal light cycles carefully to avoid excessively long vegetative periods, which can result in oversized plants that are harder to manage. One technique that outdoor growers can use is light deprivation. By covering the plants with a black tarp to artificially reduce the daylight hours, you can induce flowering earlier than the natural cycle would allow (*Best Light Schedule for Cannabis in the Flowering Stage | Fast Buds*, n.d.). However, this requires a structure like a greenhouse to be effective and manageable.

Monitoring Trichome Development

Trichomes are tiny, glandular structures that play a crucial role in determining the maturity and potency of cannabis plants. These hair-like appendages are predominantly found on the surface of cannabis flowers, but they can also be present on leaves and stems. Understanding trichomes is essential for growers aiming to cultivate high-quality cannabis, as these structures contain the majority of the plant's cannabinoids, terpenes, and other important compounds.

There are three main types of trichomes: bulbous, capitate-sessile, and capitate-stalked. Bulbous trichomes are the smallest and least significant in terms of cannabinoid production. They appear as tiny bumps on the plant's surface but do not contribute much to its overall potency. Capitate-sessile trichomes are slightly larger and have a more substantial cannabinoid content. However, the most critical type for growers are the capitate-stalked trichomes. These are the largest trichomes, easily visible under magnification, and they house the highest concentrations of cannabinoids and terpenes. They consist of a stalk and a gland head, where the resin is produced and stored.

As cannabis plants mature, the color of their trichomes undergoes noticeable changes, serving as a visual cue for harvest timing. Initially, trichomes are clear and transparent, indicating that the cannabinoids inside are still in their early stages of development. During this phase, harvesting the plant would result in lower potency and yield. As the trichomes continue to mature, they turn milky white or cloudy. This stage is often considered ideal for harvesting by many growers because it signifies peak cannabinoid production. The compounds within the trichomes are at their most potent, providing the desired effects and therapeutic benefits.

Eventually, some trichomes will turn amber or gold, indicating further maturation. At this point, the THC content starts to degrade into cannabinol (CBN), which produces more sedative effects. Growers targeting specific effects or using cannabis for medical purposes might prefer harvesting when trichomes are partly amber to achieve a balance between potency and relaxation. On the other hand, if the majority of the trichomes have turned dark amber or gold, this suggests over-maturation, which can lead to a reduction in overall quality and potency. Therefore, understanding these color changes and their implications helps growers make informed decisions about the best time to harvest. (*Trichomes Unveiled: Decoding Cannabis Maturity and Quality for Improved Cannabis Production*, 2023)

Monitoring trichome development requires specific tools to ensure accurate assessment without damaging the plant. One of the simplest and most accessible tools is the jeweler's loupe, which provides magnification levels ranging from 10x to 30x. By using a loupe, growers can closely inspect the shape and color of the trichomes without needing advanced equipment. Another popular tool is the handheld microscope, which offers higher magnification (up to 100x) and allows for a more detailed examination of trichome heads. Digital microscopes connected to computers or smartphones provide even greater clarity and the ability to capture images for further analysis and comparison.

Using these tools effectively involves gentle handling of the cannabis buds to avoid breaking off delicate trichomes. Growers typically start with a naked-eye inspection to look for the glittery appearance indicating a healthy presence of trichomes. Following this, they use a jeweler's loupe or handheld microscope to zoom in on the trichomes' color and structure. Regular inspections, particularly as the plant approaches its expected harvest time, help growers track the progression of trichome development and plan the optimal harvest window.

To accurately monitor trichome growth over time, it is crucial to conduct routine checks weekly or bi-weekly, especially during the flowering phase. Keeping a log or journal of observations, including the date and trichome status, can help growers predict how quickly the trichomes are maturing and make timely decisions for harvesting. Consistency in monitoring ensures that growers can sync the harvest with the peak potency of cannabinoids and terpenes.

Harvest timing decisions are not solely based on trichome color; they also consider factors such as strain genetics and user preferences. Different cannabis strains may exhibit distinct trichome development timelines, influenced by their genetic makeup. Some strains may never turn fully amber, while others might reach this stage faster. Understanding the specific characteristics of the strain being cultivated enables growers to align their harvesting strategies with the plant's natural development cycle. (*What Are Cannabis Trichomes? An Overview + Growing Tips*, n.d.)

User preferences also play a significant role in determining the optimal harvest time. Medical cannabis patients might prioritize harvesting during the milky trichome stage to maximize therapeutic benefits, while recreational users might prefer a mix of milky and amber trichomes for balanced psychoactive effects. Additionally, some users might aim for specific terpene profiles that are present at different stages of trichome maturity, further influencing the decision-making process.

Balancing trichome development with personal preferences involves a nuanced understanding of how trichomes impact the final product's quality and effects. For example, harvesting at the early milky stage could preserve more of the uplifting and energizing effects of THC, making it suitable for daytime use. In contrast, waiting until more trichomes turn amber can enhance the calming and sedative properties, better suited for nighttime use.

By considering both trichome indicators and user needs, growers can fine-tune their harvest timing to produce cannabis that meets specific goals and preferences. This approach ensures that the product not only delivers the desired effects but also maintains high potency and quality.

Final Analysis

Recognizing the start of the flowering phase and monitoring trichome development are essential steps for achieving a successful cannabis harvest. By observing changes such as the emergence of pistils, stretching, and alterations in light cycles, growers can tailor their care routines to ensure plants thrive. Additionally, understanding the role of trichomes and their color changes provides crucial insights into the best harvest time.

Clear trichomes indicate early stages, milky white suggests peak potency, and amber signals over-maturation. Using tools like jeweler's loupes and handheld microscopes, growers can make informed decisions based on these visual cues.

Balancing harvest timing with personal goals allows hobbyist gardeners, medical cannabis patients, and recreational users to achieve desired effects and benefits. Whether aiming for uplifting daytime use or calming nighttime relief, careful observation and routine checks help sync the harvest with peak cannabinoid and terpene levels. This chapter emphasizes that success in cannabis cultivation lies in paying attention to these key indicators and adjusting practices accordingly. Understanding these nuances not only enhances the quality of the final product but also enriches the overall growing experience.

Reference List

Best Light Schedule For Cannabis In The Flowering Stage | Fast Buds . (n.d.). 2fast4buds.com. Retrieved August 2, 2024, from https://2fast4buds.com/news/best-light-schedule-for-cannabis-in-the-flowering-stage

Trichomes Unveiled: Decoding Cannabis Maturity and Quality for Improved Cannabis Production . (2023, December 12). LSU AgCenter. https://www.lsuagcenter.com/articles/page1702395856798

The Stages of Cannabis Growth | CleanLeaf Blog . (n.d.). Cleanleaf.com. https://cleanleaf.com/the-stages-of-cannabis-growth.php

What are Cannabis Trichomes? An Overview + Growing Tips . (n.d.). SunMed Growers. Retrieved August 2, 2024, from https://www.sunmedgrowers.com/education-resources/blog/post/cannabis-trichomes/

Chapter Eleven

Harvesting and Curing

Harvesting and curing cannabis are crucial steps that directly influence the potency, flavor, and overall quality of the final product. Getting these processes right ensures that all the hard work put into growing cannabis pays off with a top-quality harvest. The timing of when to cut down your plants can make or break the entire growing operation. Too early, and the buds might not reach their full potential; too late, and they could lose their potency and flavor. Observing the color and condition of the trichomes helps growers determine the perfect moment for harvesting, ensuring they capture the maximum cannabinoid levels at their peak.

In this chapter, we'll delve into the essential techniques for harvesting your cannabis plants, including the use of proper tools to avoid damaging them. We'll also explore different trimming methods, such as hand trimming and the choice between wet and dry trimming, each with its unique advantages. Moreover, we'll discuss the importance of handling your freshly cut plants gently to preserve the valuable trichomes and resin. This chapter will guide you through every meticulous step of the process, from cutting and trimming to drying and curing, ensuring you achieve the best results for your cannabis crop.

Cutting, Trimming, and Handling Plants

Timing of Harvesting

The timing of harvesting cannabis is a crucial factor that significantly impacts the final product's quality. To achieve optimal potency and flavor, growers need to master the art of timing their harvest correctly. Harvesting too early can result in buds that lack the desired cannabinoid content, leading to a less potent product. Conversely, harvesting too late can cause the cannabinoids to degrade, diminishing both the potency and flavor.

One of the key indicators for determining the right time to harvest is observing the color of the trichomes, which are the tiny, resinous glands on the cannabis flowers. Trichomes contain the highest concentration of cannabinoids, including THC and CBD. By monitoring these trichomes, growers can get a clear idea of whether their crop is ready for harvest. When trichomes are clear, it indicates that the plant needs more time to mature. As they turn milky white, this signals peak cannabinoid levels, making it the ideal time to harvest. Amber-colored trichomes suggest that the plant might be past its prime, with some degradation in potency but potentially a different effect profile.

Tools for Harvesting

Effective harvesting demands the use of proper tools. The right equipment ensures that the plants are not damaged during the process, maintaining their overall health and quality. Sharp, clean scissors or shears are essential tools for cutting and trimming cannabis. Using sharp blades minimizes any tearing or crushing of the stems, which can lead to unnecessary stress on the plants. A clean cut reduces the risk of introducing disease or pests, as jagged edges can become entry points for pathogens.

Another essential aspect of using proper tools is hygiene. Tools should be sterilized before each use to prevent cross-contamination between plants. Simple practices like wiping down the scissors with alcohol can go a long way in maintaining plant health. Familiarity with these tools also contributes to a smoother and more efficient harvesting process, allowing growers to work quickly and effectively without causing undue harm to their plants.

Trimming Techniques

Once the cannabis plants have been harvested, the next step is trimming. This involves removing excess leaves and improving the appearance of the buds. Effective trimming techniques not only enhance the visual appeal but also contribute to the overall quality of the product. There are various styles of trimming, each with its own benefits.

Hand trimming is considered one of the most precise methods. Using a pair of sharp, clean trimming scissors, carefully trim away any large fan leaves that overshadow the buds. Trim closely to the base of the buds, removing unnecessary foliage that may hinder airflow or contain minimal trichomes. Sugar leaf trimming involves targeting the small leaves that grow around the buds. Carefully trimming these leaves close to the bud improves appearance and smoking experience by leaving behind only those with abundant trichome coverage (*Trimming and Pruning: Enhancing Quality during Cannabis Harvesting*, n.d.).

There is also the decision between wet and dry trimming. Wet trimming is done when the buds are fresh and moist, making it easier to manipulate the buds but potentially messier and with an increased risk of mold. Dry trimming requires more delicacy but preserves trichomes better. Choosing the right technique depends on balancing the preservation of trichomes and achieving an aesthetically pleasing final product.

Handling the Cut Plants

Proper handling of freshly cut cannabis plants is vital to preserving their quality throughout the drying and curing process. Gentle handling helps preserve the delicate trichomes and resin that are concentrated on the buds. Mishandling can easily knock off these valuable compounds, reducing the potency and impact of the final product.

One key practice is careful placement during drying. It's important to hang the plants or place them on drying racks in a manner that prevents unwanted bruising. Avoid stacking the plants too closely together, as this can create pressure points that damage the buds. Instead, ensure there is ample space for airflow, which aids in even drying and prevents mold formation.

Proper handling techniques extend into the curing phase as well. By maintaining a gentle touch and careful placement, growers help preserve the flavor and potency of the cannabis through to the final stages. The cumulative effect of meticulous handling at every stage of the process results in a superior product that retains its desired characteristics.

Drying and Curing Methods

Drying and curing cannabis are crucial steps in ensuring the best possible quality, potency, and flavor of your harvest. Different methods have distinct impacts on the final product, so it's essential to understand and implement these techniques effectively. Let's explore some common drying and curing methods and how they influence cannabis characteristics.

Air Drying serves as a traditional and widely-used method for drying cannabis. This technique involves hanging trimmed buds upside down in a dark, well-ventilated area. Slow drying through air drying retains terpenes, which are responsible for the plant's aroma and flavor. By avoiding rapid temperature fluctuations, this method also helps prevent the loss of potency. Adequate airflow during the drying process is critical to prevent mold growth. Placing fans strategically around the drying space ensures proper circulation without blowing directly onto the buds, which can lead to over-drying or uneven moisture levels. Familiarity with humidity levels plays a significant role in achieving optimal drying outcomes. Maintaining an environment with a relative humidity of around 50-60% allows the buds to dry slowly and evenly. Investing in a hygrometer to monitor humidity levels can be particularly beneficial in managing the drying conditions meticulously.

Using Drying Racks is another effective method for cannabis drying. These racks provide a structured approach to drying by utilizing horizontal mesh trays stacked vertically. The primary advantage of drying racks is their ability to allow even air circulation around the buds, preventing bud compression and maintaining the integrity of delicate trichomes. Proper use of drying racks involves spreading the buds uniformly on each tray, ensuring ample spacing between individual flowers for optimal airflow. Vertical space utilization enhances drying efficiency, especially when dealing with larger harvests in limited spaces. Rotating the trays periodically can further promote consistent drying across all sections. Knowledge of rack placements within the drying room aids in creating an optimal drying environment. Placing the racks in a cool, dark, and well-ventilated area minimizes exposure to light, heat, and excessive moisture, which can degrade cannabinoid content and overall quality.

The duration of the curing process significantly influences the final quality of the cannabis. Curing typically follows the initial drying phase and involves storing the dried buds in airtight containers to continue the maturation process. Longer curing times can develop richer flavor profiles and smoother smoke. Extended curing allows enzymatic processes within the buds to break down residual sugars, starches, and chlorophyll, resulting in a more refined end product. Regular monitoring of moisture balance is essential during this period. Buds that are too wet can develop mold, while overly dry buds lose their potency and flavor. Checking the buds periodically and feeling them can help determine if adjustments are needed. Understanding individual strains can guide curing times effectively. Some strains benefit from shorter curing periods, while others may require several months to reach their full potential. Experimentation and keen observation will help find the ideal curing duration for each specific strain.

Burping Jars is a technique used during the curing process to manage moisture levels within the storage containers. Burping involves periodically opening the jars to release built-up moisture and allow fresh air to circulate. This practice ensures that excess moisture does not accumulate, which is vital for preventing mold growth while retaining the buds' flavor. The general guideline for burping is to open the jars daily for 30 minutes during the first week of curing. As the curing process progresses, the frequency of burping can be reduced gradually. By the second week, burp the jars every other day, and by the third week, only once every few days. Sensory cues, such as smell and feel, play a crucial role in determining the necessity of burping. If the buds feel excessively moist or have a musty odor, it may indicate the need for more frequent burping. Conversely, if the buds feel dry and crispy, reducing the burping frequency might be required. Techniques for determining when burping is necessary rely heavily on observation and experience. A small digital hygrometer placed inside the jars can provide constant readings of relative humidity, offering precision in maintaining the ideal curing environment. Aim to keep the humidity levels within a range of 55-65% to strike a balance between preventing mold and preserving the desired characteristics of the cannabis.

Lessons Learned

In this chapter, we've delved into the essentials of properly harvesting and curing cannabis to ensure top-notch quality. From understanding the perfect timing by observing trichomes to selecting the right tools and mastering trimming techniques, we've covered the key steps that significantly impact potency, flavor, and overall results.

By handling the plants with care during the drying and curing process, growers can preserve the delicate trichomes and resin that contribute to the plant's therapeutic and recreational benefits.

As you implement these methods, remember that meticulous attention to detail pays off in the end. Proper timing, careful handling, and effective drying and curing help maintain the plant's integrity, leading to a superior product. Whether you're growing for medicinal purposes or personal enjoyment, these techniques will guide you to achieve the best possible outcome from your harvest.

Reference List

Cannabis Curing Techniques: Exploring Different Methods for Optimal Results . (n.d.). Floraflex.com. Retrieved August 2, 2024, from https://floraflex.com/default/blog/post/cannabis-curing-techniques-exploring-different-methods-for-optimal-results

How and Why to Burp Your Weed - RQS Blog . (n.d.). Royal Queen Seeds. Retrieved August 2, 2024, from https://www.royalqueenseeds.com/us/blog-how-and-why-to-burp-your-weed-n1492

Pruning Cannabis to Promote Growth and Health . (n.d.). SunMed Growers. Retrieved August 2, 2024, from https://www.sunmedgrowers.com/education-resources/blog/post/the-art-of-pruning-cannabis/

Trimming and Pruning: Enhancing Quality During Cannabis Harvesting . (n.d.). Floraflex.com. Retrieved August 2, 2024, from https://floraflex.com/default/blog/post/trimming-and-pruning-enhancing-quality-during-cannabis-harvesting

Chapter Twelve

Safe Usage and Legal Considerations

Safe usage and legal considerations of cannabis involve much more than just knowing the difference between medical and recreational uses. It's about being equipped with the right knowledge to make informed choices, ensuring both personal safety and adherence to legal frameworks. Understanding how cannabis can be responsibly used, whether it's for managing medical conditions or for leisure, starts with recognizing that each form of use has its own set of regulations and societal perceptions.

In this chapter, we'll navigate through the intricacies of using cannabis responsibly, highlighting essential practices for safe consumption. We will delve into the importance of consulting healthcare professionals for medical usage and understanding personal limits for recreational use. Additionally, we'll explore the various legal landscapes governing cannabis across different regions, providing you with critical insights to avoid legal pitfalls. Whether you're a medical patient seeking relief, a hobbyist gardener curious about cultivation, or someone interested in the wellness benefits of cannabis, this chapter will guide you through safe and ethical engagement with the plant.

Medical vs. Recreational Use

When diving into the world of cannabis, one must understand the distinctions between medical and recreational use and the implications of each. Medical cannabis is often prescribed by healthcare providers to manage specific ailments such as chronic pain, epilepsy, and certain psychological conditions. These medical uses are grounded in scientific research that underscores cannabis's potential therapeutic benefits. On the other hand, recreational cannabis is typically consumed for enjoyment, relaxation, and social purposes. While both forms of cannabis come from the same plant, their intended uses and the contexts in which they are consumed differ greatly.

From a legal perspective, understanding these differences is crucial. The legal definitions and regulations surrounding medical and recreational cannabis vary significantly across states and countries. For instance, some states have legalized both medical and recreational cannabis, while others have strict regulations permitting only medical use under specific conditions. Additionally, cannabis remains illegal under federal law in many places, adding another layer of complexity. This patchwork of laws necessitates that users familiarize themselves with the regulations in their respective areas to ensure compliance and avoid legal ramifications. Whether you're considering cannabis for medical or recreational purposes, it's imperative to stay informed about the local laws governing its use.

Social perceptions also play a significant role in shaping how medical and recreational cannabis are viewed. Recreational use often carries a stigma, partly due to historical portrayals of cannabis users and long-standing legal prohibitions. Many people associate recreational cannabis use with negative stereotypes, which can influence public opinion and policy. Conversely, medical cannabis has gained more legitimacy and acceptance, particularly as more studies highlight its potential health benefits. Patients using cannabis for medical reasons are often seen as seeking relief rather than indulging in a recreational activity. This shift in perception underscores the importance of educating the public about the legitimate therapeutic uses of cannabis and dispelling myths surrounding its consumption.

When it comes to choosing cannabis products responsibly, whether for medical or recreational use, several practical considerations should be taken into account. First and foremost, consulting a healthcare professional is paramount, especially for medical cannabis users. A healthcare provider can help determine the appropriate strains, dosages, and methods of consumption tailored to individual health needs. They can also monitor potential interactions with other medications and manage any side effects. For recreational users, responsible consumption involves understanding your own limits and opting for products that align with your personal preferences and tolerance levels.

Selecting the right cannabis product involves evaluating various factors, such as potency, dosage forms, and purity. Potency can vary widely between products, with some designed to deliver high levels of THC (tetrahydrocannabinol) for intense effects, while others may contain higher CBD (cannabidiol) levels, offering a milder experience. Dosage forms include smokable flower, edibles, tinctures, and topicals, each with different onset times and durations of effect. It's essential to start with lower doses, especially for new users, to gauge how your body reacts and prevent overconsumption.

Purity and quality control are also critical aspects. Reputable dispensaries provide lab-tested products, ensuring they are free from harmful contaminants like pesticides and heavy metals. Labels should clearly indicate the cannabinoid content and provide detailed information about the product's origins. When possible, opt for products with a certificate of analysis, which guarantees that the cannabis has been tested for safety and potency by an independent laboratory.

Finally, it's important to acknowledge the broader societal impacts of cannabis use. Responsible consumption extends beyond individual decisions and encompasses considering the effects on communities and public health. Overuse or misuse of cannabis can lead to adverse outcomes such as impaired driving or substance dependence. Public education campaigns and community programs play a vital role in promoting safe practices and reducing potential harms associated with cannabis consumption.

Effects, Side Effects, and Dosage Guidelines

Cannabis induces a range of effects, largely dependent on the levels of THC (tetrahydrocannabinol) and CBD (cannabidiol) present in the strain. THC is primarily responsible for the psychoactive properties, producing feelings of euphoria, relaxation, or stimulation. High-THC strains are commonly sought after for their potent euphoric and stimulating effects. However, they can sometimes lead to heightened anxiety or paranoia, especially in first-time users or those sensitive to THC. On the other hand, CBD does not produce a high but can mitigate some of THC's adverse effects, such as anxiety and paranoia, promoting a more balanced experience. Cannabis strains with higher CBD content are often appreciated for their calming and therapeutic benefits without intense psychoactive effects.

It is crucial to understand that individual responses to cannabis can vary significantly. Factors such as body weight, metabolism, tolerance, and even the individual's mental state at the time of consumption play a role in how one experiences cannabis. Starting with small doses is highly recommended, particularly for new users. This approach, popularly known as "start low, go slow," allows individuals to find their personal thresholds and minimize the risk of unwanted side effects. For example, beginning with a low-THC strain and gradually increasing the amount can help in gauging one's comfort level and avoid overwhelming experiences.

Common side effects of cannabis include anxiety, dry mouth, dizziness, and increased heart rate. While these side effects are generally mild and temporary, they can be uncomfortable. Strategies to mitigate these side effects are beneficial. Staying hydrated can help manage dry mouth, while taking breaks between consumption can reduce dizziness and prevent overconsumption. If experiencing anxiety, opting for a strain with higher CBD content can provide a more relaxing experience. It is also important to consume cannabis in a comfortable and familiar environment, reducing the likelihood of anxiety.

Different methods of cannabis consumption influence both dosage and effects. Smoking or vaping provides rapid onset of effects, making it easier to control the dosage due to its immediate impact. This method is suitable for those who prefer quick relief, such as medical cannabis users seeking pain management. However, smoking may irritate the lungs and airways, prompting some to explore alternatives like edibles or tinctures.

Edibles, which involve ingesting cannabis-infused products like brownies or gummies, can have delayed and prolonged effects. The onset can take anywhere from 30 minutes to 2 hours, and the duration can extend for several hours. Due to this delay, it is easy to overconsume, leading to intense and prolonged effects. Therefore, it is essential to start with a small portion and wait at least two hours before considering additional intake. Tinctures, typically administered sublingually, offer a middle ground with quicker onset than edibles but longer duration than smoking. They allow for precise dosing, which is particularly helpful for medical cannabis patients needing consistent effects.

In addition to understanding one's reaction to various strains and methods of consumption, seeking professional guidance can be highly valuable. Consulting healthcare providers who are knowledgeable about cannabis can help tailor recommendations based on individual health conditions and goals. They can provide insights into safe dosages and potential interactions with other medications. This is particularly important for medical cannabis users who rely on the plant to manage chronic conditions such as pain, multiple sclerosis, or nausea induced by chemotherapy.

Legal limits also play a crucial role in ensuring safe usage. Different regions have varying regulations regarding the purchase, possession, and consumption of cannabis. Being aware of these local laws not only helps avoid legal repercussions but also promotes responsible use. For instance, many places limit the quantity of cannabis that individuals can possess or cultivate at home. Adhering to these limits is important to ensure compliance with the law and community standards.

Educational resources are invaluable in navigating the complexities surrounding cannabis use. Books, online courses, and workshops provide in-depth knowledge about safe consumption practices, strain selection, and legal considerations. These resources can empower users to make informed decisions and promote a culture of responsible use. For hobbyist gardeners, educational materials can introduce advanced cultivation techniques, enhancing the quality and yield of home-grown cannabis. Medical cannabis patients can benefit from tailored guidance on selecting strains best suited for their symptoms, understanding the nuances of different consumption methods, and integrating cannabis into their overall treatment plan.

It's also beneficial to connect with local growers and support groups. Engaging with experienced cultivators can provide practical insights and tips that are not always covered in written materials. Support groups offer a platform for sharing experiences, challenges, and successes, fostering a sense of community among cannabis users. Whether for medical, recreational, or wellness purposes, having a supportive network can enhance the overall experience and encourage responsible use.

Local workshops and seminars are excellent opportunities to deepen one's understanding of cannabis. These events often feature experts in the field, covering topics ranging from cultivation techniques to emerging research on cannabis' therapeutic benefits. Attending these sessions can provide practical hands-on knowledge and keep users updated on the latest advancements and trends in the cannabis industry. Online resources, although vast, need to be approached cautiously. Not all information found online is accurate or applicable. Relying on reputable websites, academic journals, and official publications ensures that the information is credible and reliable. Participating in online forums and discussion groups can also be beneficial, as long as users are discerning about the sources of advice and recommendations.

In summary, responsible cannabis use involves understanding the various effects of THC and CBD, starting with low doses to discover personal limits, and being aware of common side effects and mitigation strategies. Different consumption methods require specific precautions to ensure safe and enjoyable experiences. Seeking professional guidance, adhering to legal limits, and utilizing educational resources can further enhance safe usage. Engaging with the community through workshops and support groups can provide additional support and foster a culture of responsible cannabis use. By equipping themselves with this knowledge, readers can confidently navigate the world of cannabis, whether for medical, recreational, or personal wellness purposes.

Final Insights

In this chapter, we've explored the crucial aspects of using cannabis responsibly by distinguishing between its medical and recreational uses. Understanding these differences helps ensure that you approach the plant safely and ethically, whether seeking therapeutic benefits or simply looking to relax. We've delved into how legal frameworks vary across regions, emphasizing the importance of staying informed about local laws to avoid any legal repercussions.

We've also covered practical considerations for choosing the right cannabis products, highlighting the need for consultation with healthcare professionals and starting with lower doses. By considering factors like potency, dosage forms, and purity, you can make well-informed decisions tailored to your needs. Additionally, we've discussed the broader impact of cannabis use on society, underlining the role of education in promoting safe practices. With this knowledge, you can engage with cannabis confidently and responsibly, ensuring a positive experience for yourself and your community.

Reference List

Black, L. (2022, July 14). *The Key Differences Between Medical & Recreational Weed* . GoodRx. https://www.goodrx.com/classes/cannabinoids/medicinal-vs-recreational-weed-marijuana

Lin, L. A., Ilgen, M. A., Jannausch, M., & Bohnert, K. M. (2016, October). *Comparing adults who use cannabis medically with those who use recreationally: Results from a national sample* . Addictive Behaviors. https://doi.org/10.1016/j.addbeh.2016.05.015

National Academies of Sciences, Engineering, and Medicine. (2017). *Therapeutic Effects of Cannabis and Cannabinoids* . Nih.gov; National Academies Press (US). https://www.ncbi.nlm.nih.gov/books/NBK425767/

WebMD. (2019). *Cannabis: Uses, Side Effects, Interactions, Dosage, and Warning* . Webmd.com. https://www.webmd.com/vitamins/ai/ingredientmono-947/cannabis

Chapter Thirteen

Conclusion

Throughout this guide, we have taken you from the initial understanding of cannabis cultivation to the rewarding moment of harvesting your hard work. Whether you're experimenting with indoor setups or outdoor techniques, the knowledge shared will empower you to grow cannabis with confidence. We've delved into the basics of growing cannabis, from seed selection and soil preparation to lighting and watering techniques. You've learned how to choose the right strain for your needs, whether you're aiming for medicinal benefits, recreational enjoyment, or simply exploring a new gardening challenge.

Remember, successful cannabis cultivation hinges on two main pillars: understanding your plants' biological needs and maintaining a nurturing environment. As you've learned, these fundamentals will set the stage for strong, healthy growth. You've been introduced to the importance of light cycles, nutrient management, pest control, and pruning techniques, all of which play a crucial role in ensuring that your plants reach their full potential. The journey of growing cannabis is complex and rewarding, offering both challenges and triumphs at every stage of the process.

It's essential to keep in mind the critical lessons and practices that every aspiring cannabis cultivator should remember. First and foremost, patience is key. Cannabis plants don't grow overnight; they require time, attention, and care. Monitor their progress regularly, and be proactive in addressing any issues that arise, whether it's a nutrient deficiency or a pest invasion. Cultivation is truly an ongoing learning experience, and each crop will teach you something new about the intricacies of the plant.

Another significant takeaway is the importance of creating a suitable environment for your cannabis plants. This includes regulating temperature, humidity, and airflow to mimic the plant's natural conditions as closely as possible. Paying attention to these details can mean the difference between a thriving garden and one that's struggling to survive. Equally important is staying vigilant about pests and diseases, which can quickly undermine even the best-laid plans. Implementing preventive measures and responding swiftly to any signs of trouble are critical aspects of successful cultivation.

Growing cannabis is as much an art as it is a science. Stay curious and open to new information, whether through community workshops, online forums, or local grow shops, so you can refine your approach and improve your yields. The cannabis cultivation community is a rich resource of shared experiences and expertise that can help you overcome obstacles and optimize your growing techniques. Keep learning and adapting your methods based on your personal experiences and the evolving knowledge within the cannabis community. Don't be afraid to experiment with different growing mediums, training techniques, or feeding schedules to see what works best for your specific situation.

As you continue to grow and harvest cannabis, you'll likely discover preferences for certain strains, growing methods, and consumption techniques. These personal insights will become invaluable as you fine-tune your approach and strive to achieve even better results with each subsequent crop. Documenting your processes and outcomes can also be beneficial, providing a record of what worked well and what might need adjustment in the future.

Furthermore, as you embark on your cannabis cultivation journey, always remember the importance of responsible use and legal awareness. Being informed about your local laws and regulations is not only a matter of compliance but also a way to ensure that your efforts remain safe and enjoyable. Each region has its own set of rules governing the cultivation, possession, and consumption of cannabis, and staying abreast of these regulations will help you avoid unnecessary complications.

Responsible consumption is equally important. Whether using cannabis for medicinal purposes, wellness, or recreation, moderation and mindfulness are key. Understand the potency of your plants and how different strains affect you personally. Share your harvest with others responsibly, ensuring that everyone enjoys the benefits of cannabis safely and legally.

Looking ahead, the future of cannabis cultivation holds exciting possibilities. With ongoing research and advancements in growing technologies, new strains and methods are continually being developed. Staying connected with the broader cannabis community will help you stay informed about these innovations and integrate them into your own practices. Whether it's adopting new organic fertilizers, exploring advanced hydroponic systems, or trying out novel training techniques, there are always new frontiers to explore in the world of cannabis cultivation.

In conclusion, the journey of growing cannabis is a deeply rewarding endeavor that offers numerous benefits, from the satisfaction of cultivating your own plants to the joy of discovering their various uses. As you apply the knowledge gained from this guide, remember to keep learning, adapting, and growing both your skills and your garden. The world of cannabis cultivation is vast and ever-changing, full of opportunities for those willing to nurture their curiosity and dedication.

May your cannabis garden flourish, bringing you both pleasure and purpose in the years to come. Enjoy the process, respect the plant, and embrace the community of fellow growers who share your passion. Happy gardening!

Made in the USA
Columbia, SC
11 June 2025

59198102R00046